MAKING YOUR OWN
CARDS

LYNDA WATTS

NEW
HOLLAND

First published in the UK in 1993 by
New Holland (Publishers) Ltd
24 Nutford Place, London W1H 6DQ

Reprinted in 1994 and 1995

ISBN 1 85368 178 4 (hbk)
ISBN 1 85368 239 X (pbk)

Creative editor Pauline Butler
Art director Jane Forster
Photographer Shona Wood
Illustrator Terry Evans
Calligrapher David Harris
Design assistant Sarah Willis

Phototypeset by Ace Filmsetting Ltd, Frome,
Somerset
Reproduction by Scantrans Pte Ltd, Singapore
Printed and bound in Singapore by Kyodo-Shing
Loong Printing Industries Pte Ltd

Contents

Introduction 8

CHAPTER ONE
Getting Started 11

CHAPTER TWO
Greetings 17
Thank you with flowers 18   Spotted dinosaur 20
Sleepy lion puppet card 22   Moving home 24
Bon voyage 26   Happy birthday cake 28
Country-style roses 30   Good luck 31

CHAPTER THREE
With Love 32
Sweetheart 34   Valentine hearts 36
Sorry! 38   Mother's day 40

CHAPTER FOUR
Congratulations 43
Lovebirds 44   Golden anniversary card 46
Baby bootees 48   Well done! 50

CHAPTER FIVE
Invitations 53
Origami summer invitation 54   3-D découpage place setting cards 56
Apple invitation card 58   Something special 60
Cheers! 62   Stepping out 64
Sharp dressing 66

CHAPTER SIX
Seasonal Greetings 69
Easter lamb greetings 70   Springtime pansy basket 72
Frosty landscape 74   Christmas cracker 76
Novelty Christmas tree 78

CHAPTER SEVEN
Basic Techniques 81

Useful addresses 92
Index 93

Introduction

Inspiration and design ideas for making cards can come from all sorts of unlikely sources, and my aim has been to create a book which draws on these, as well as on a variety of papercraft techniques in such a way that even those who feel they have no particular artistic flair can produce attractive and professional-looking results.

Handmade cards are always a delight to give or receive, and some are special enough to want to keep for ever – whether the message is a simple 'hello' or an invitation to a never-to-be-forgotten occasion.

Once you start making your own cards, keep your eyes open all the time for new ideas and materials, for often an image seen in a magazine or store can spark off an idea for an unusual design. While planning the designs in this book I deliberately chose elements which did not require drawing skills. Pattern shapes and templates used for crafts like embroidery and patchwork can be adapted to provide original, clearly defined images, while dressmaking trimmings and stationery products can often add the important little details which bring a design to life. Children's story books and colouring books can also provide useful source material, as many have simple, stylized pictures of animals, buildings or plants, which you can easily just trace and re-position as desired.

The card designs range from those made simply by folding a piece of card in half and adding decorations, to more complicated images where the card shape itself forms an integral part of the design. The designs also draw on a variety of techniques, from simple paper folding to origami and 3-D découpage. Some of the methods used will already be familiar to you, but there should also be plenty of new ones for everyone to try.

Although the cards are divided into different chapter headings, many of the designs are suitable for more than one occasion, and the basic instructions should provide you with enough confidence to create your own variations, or at least to adapt a card suggested for one occasion for an alternative event. By experimenting, and with a little imagination, you can make truly individual cards using the new skills you have acquired or forgotten skills reawakened from childhood days – so do let your imagination work for you, as you can achieve truly creative results.

Follow the step-by-step instructions and illustrations to help you get the best results from your endeavours. Look at the **Getting Started** chapter for information on choosing papers, materials and equipment, and at the **Basic Techniques** chapter for tips and basic know-how on preparing paper and card and transferring designs. This chapter also shows you how to work quick 3-D découpage, quilling (paper filigree) and paper folds for origami designs. Templates and pattern diagrams are also given here, as are instructions for making those vital finishing touches – envelopes. Two pattern styles are included for these, and either one can be adapted to fit any size or style of greetings card.

The materials required are listed at the beginning of each project – but you can experiment and substitute other materials. Just make sure you choose alternatives in an equal weight to those suggested so that they handle in a similar way.

Finally, remember that you do not have to be an 'artist' to make interesting cards, it is only necessary to be creative, and to be enthusiastic about attempting new projects and developing fresh skills.

Chapter 1
Getting started

Most of the materials recommended are quite basic, and you should have little problem purchasing or ordering them from local stores, stationery shops and art and craft suppliers. You may already have many of the materials necessary for making your own cards, so it can be a relatively inexpensive hobby. However, certain items are necessary to do a job well, and to produce professional-looking results.

Papers

Throughout the book the main material used is paper. This is a wonderfully versatile material, and it is readily available in a seemingly endless range of colours, textures and weights. Because of this diversity, it is important to recognize and understand some of the basic qualities of paper in order to select the most appropriate kind for a particular project.

The requirements section at the beginning of each project suggests suitable papers for the job, so follow this advice in order to achieve a reliable finish. However, if you would like to try an alternative type of paper, just experiment, and trust to good luck. Although your results may sometimes be disappointing, you are likely to produce a card you can be proud of in the end – just be prepared for a varying degree of success!

When choosing paper the variety of different types and sizes can be bewildering, so the best place to look for papers and card is in an art or craft shop, or in a specialist paper shop where advice is at hand if needed. Some of these suppliers also offer a mail order service, so if you plan to make a lot of cards, it is worth investigating these sources.

When designing your own cards, try to find a paper with a finish or texture that is somehow appropriate to the subject matter, as this will greatly enhance the effect. Paper and card are available with textured, mottled, metallic, glossy or matt finishes. Particularly useful artist's papers include different grades of watercolour paper, and colourful Canson and cover papers. All of these have attractive surface textures and handle well. Craft papers include stretchy crêpe and double crêpe papers, tissue papers, as well as plain and patterned papers for special crafts like origami and narrow paper strips for paper filigree work. Giftwrap papers and foils also offer a good choice of pattern and texture, and many of these can be used to create interesting backgrounds or details on card designs. Handmade papers made from flowers and plants, or subtle Oriental papers and gold-printed Italian papers or marbled papers are very beautiful, and can create the perfect background or finishing touch to a simple card design. It is worth remembering that although some of these specialist papers are expensive, a little

Greetings cards can be made from a very wide range of papers and card. Choose from colourful art papers, beautiful handmade papers decorated with leaf and flower fragments, glossy foils and delicate tissue papers.

goes a long way and the result could be well worth the outlay!

Besides the coloured and decorative papers used to make the cards, you will need 'working' papers in the form of tracing paper, graph paper and typing or copy paper. These papers are used for transferring designs, making patterns and strengthening other papers.

Storing paper: Whenever possible, try to store paper flat. If you do not have a drawer deep enough for this, make a simple portfolio from two sheets of strong card, both slightly larger than the paper to be stored. Just place the paper between the card, and tie tapes parcel-fashion round the outside to keep the 'sandwich' flat. Alternatively, roll papers loosely, to prevent them developing a permanent curl, and protect the roll with a large sheet of brown parcel paper. Fold this over at the ends to protect the frail paper edges, and secure with a length of tape.

Knowing your paper: Paper is available in many sizes and there are various standards. However, the sizes most widely known and available are the A sizes – from the smallest size A6 up to A1.

Weight: Paper and card have two basic and important properties: weight and grain. Paper weight is usually measured in grams per square metre, abbreviated to g/m or gsm. As a general guideline, when selecting

Giftwrap papers offer enormous potential for designs too, because they come in so many different patterns and textures. Most papers are readily available, and many can be obtained from specialist suppliers.

paper, 'lightweight' includes tissue paper and some Oriental papers, 'light to middleweight' papers include general everyday papers, such as writing and copy paper, and these weigh between 80 gsm and 120 gsm. Papers from 150 gsm to 200 gsm are 'medium- to heavy-weight'. Anything over 225 gsm is classed as card. Paper that weighs over this amount is known as board. The majority of greetings cards can be made from papers weighing around 150 gsm.

Grain: The grain relates to the fibre content and make-up of the paper. The grain defines the direction in which the fibres of the paper lie. Handmade paper has no grain and its edges are rough and uneven, but all machine-made papers do have a grain. This is created during manufacture as the pulp fibres settle in the same direction as the movement of the machine belt. Grain imparts certain qualities to paper; for example, paper can be torn, curved or folded quite easily along its grain, but the lie of the fibres creates resistance when these actions are repeated against the grain. Because of this, always check the direction of the grain before you start working with a sheet of paper when pleating, curling or folding are necessary to the design.

Tools and materials

Cutting tools: A craft knife is used at some point for making almost every design in this book. It is essential that any knife is easy to handle, and has a sharp blade to ensure clean cuts. It is worth having a small, scalpel-sized knife for cutting lightweight paper and small details, and a larger household craft knife for scoring and cutting thicker paper and card. When using a knife to cut straight lines on paper and card, it is vital to have a firm straight edge to cut against. Use a steel rule for this job, as the knife blade could catch in a soft wood or plastic rule. Use craft knives over a special self-healing cutting board (available from art and graphic suppliers) or a sheet of thick cardboard, to protect work surfaces.

Ideally, work with a selection of different size sharp scissors. Embroidery scissors and curved manicure scissors are also useful; use these to cut out small shapes, and for reaching into awkward corners. Dressmaking pinking shears can also be used, to create an interesting zigzag effect on the edges of paper, card or fabric.

Other useful cutting tools are a stationery hole punch and a wad punch. The latter is a small tool which can house punch fittings for different diameter holes. Unlike other hole punches, the wad punch can be positioned wherever it is required. A smart tap with a hammer will punch a clean hole through the surface of the paper or card. Wad punches are obtainable by mail order from craft suppliers.

Adhesives: Three main types of adhesive have been used in the book: clear craft adhesive; stick adhesive; spray adhesive. Clear craft adhesive is quick-drying and can be used for most surfaces, including paper and fabric and for attaching small plastic or other lightweight trimmings. Stick adhesive is ideal for joining paper to paper –

particularly lightweight papers. Spray adhesive is available from art and graphic suppliers. This produces a fine, sticky mist so it is perfect for use on thin or delicate papers, as well as on lightweight fabrics. The advantage of this adhesive over some other types is its delayed drying time; sprayed materials can be re-positioned easily if desired. Care must be taken when using this type of adhesive, to prevent the fine particles from spoiling surrounding surfaces. The best way to control this is by making a spray booth from a large cardboard box – the item to be sprayed can be placed inside. Use the adhesive sparingly, and in a well ventilated area. When using any adhesive, follow the manufacturer's instructions carefully to avoid accidents.

Apart from normal sticky tape which is invaluable at many design stages for holding tracings in place, another useful tape is double-sided sticky tape. Use this to join paper surfaces together neatly and invisibly.

Drawing materials: A set square and ruler, a compass, an HB pencil and pencil sharpener, an eraser, coloured pencils and felt-tip pens, coloured inks.

Decorative touches: You will need a whole variety of materials for surface decoration, such as fabric, felt, ribbons and braids, gemstones, sequins, beads, thread/string, paper doilies, silk and pressed flowers. Plastic modelling clay is also useful, as it can be moulded and cut into an endless variety of decorative shapes. Take a look in your sewing box too, before buying materials as you may find trimmings and knick-knacks here which could be used to embellish cards.

Also required: Sewing needles, self-adhesive foam pads, tweezers, a quilling (paper filigree) tool.

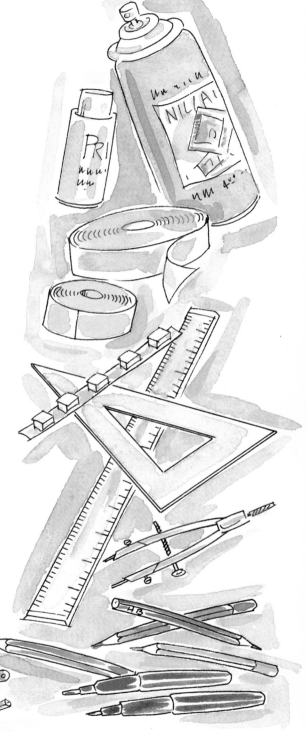

Chapter 2
Greetings

Thank you with flowers

This colourful bouquet of quilled paper flowers is a great way to say 'thank you'. Despite appearances, these flowers are quick and easy to make.

REQUIREMENTS
A sheet of white art paper (Canson paper)
A quilling tool
Strips of 10 mm wide quilling paper in red, yellow and orange
Strips of 3 mm wide quilling paper in red, yellow, orange and green
A small piece of red art paper (Canson paper)
Clear craft adhesive
A small plate for use as a template
*(See the **Basic Techniques** chapter, page 90 for more information on quilling).*

To make the flowers

1   To make a quilled flower, start with an 18 cm (7 in) length of 10 mm wide yellow quilling paper. Cut very narrow slits all the way along the strip, to within 2 mm (¹⁄₁₀ in) of the straight edge.

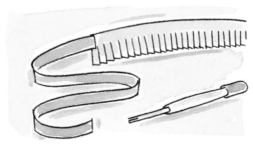

2   Put a dab of adhesive on one end of the yellow strip, close to the uncut edge, and join it to one of the 3 mm wide strips of orange quilling paper. Leave to dry.
3   Put the other end of the orange quilling paper into the slot at the top of the quilling tool and roll both strips very tightly with the quilling tool.

4   When you have rolled the strips, secure the loose end with a dab of adhesive to prevent the coil unravelling. Remove from the quilling tool and leave to dry.

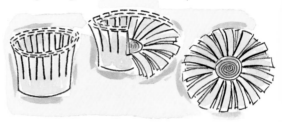

5   To finish, carefully open the fringed 'petals' and gently flatten them with your fingers to form a flower shape.
6   Repeat these steps, changing the colour sequence, until you have made nine flowers.

To make the card

1   Cut a rectangle 22 x 15 cm (8½ x 6 in) from white paper. Mark and score a fold line halfway along the longest edge.
2   To make the template for the bouquet wrapper, draw around a small plate, about 18 cm (7 in) in diameter on to a piece of scrap paper. Cut out, then divide the circle into four. Cut out one quarter and use this as the template for the wrapper.
3   Draw round the template on red paper and cut out. Fold in the side edges, so that they overlap each other. Gently stretch the overlapping curved edge over a scissor blade to give a natural curve to the wrapper opening. Stick the wrapper diagonally across the lower two-thirds of the card mount so two loose flaps are on the outside. Secure the flaps of the wrapper with adhesive.
4   Cut some short strips from green quilling paper and cut the ends into points, to make leaves. Stick some to the inside of the wrapper as a background. Curl two of the strips along scissor blades, and stick the strips, curling outwards, inside the front folds of the wrapper.
5   Put a dab of adhesive on to the back of each quilled flower and stick them to the card. Arrange them so they appear to be bursting out from the paper wrapper.
6   Cut a strip of narrow yellow quilling paper and make it into a bow to trim the front of the wrapper. Stick in place on the front of the wrapper.

Quilled flowers in shades of red, orange and yellow make up this impressive bouquet.

Spotted dinosaur

This jolly dinosaur card will add a splash of colour to a youngster's birthday celebrations. The dinosaur folds up small enough to fit into an envelope, and there is plenty of space on the back of the card for special birthday messages.

REQUIREMENTS
A sheet of thin green card
A sheet of thin yellow card
A sheet of shiny green self-adhesive paper,
    (or substitute shiny green paper and
    spray adhesive)
Tiny oddments of black and white card
Stick adhesive
*(See the **Basic Techniques** chapter, page 84*
for information on transferring patterns)

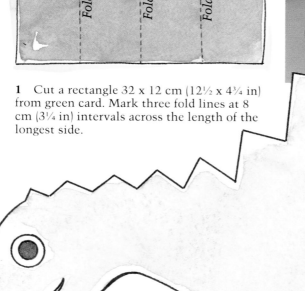

1 Cut a rectangle 32 x 12 cm (12½ x 4¾ in) from green card. Mark three fold lines at 8 cm (3¼ in) intervals across the length of the longest side.

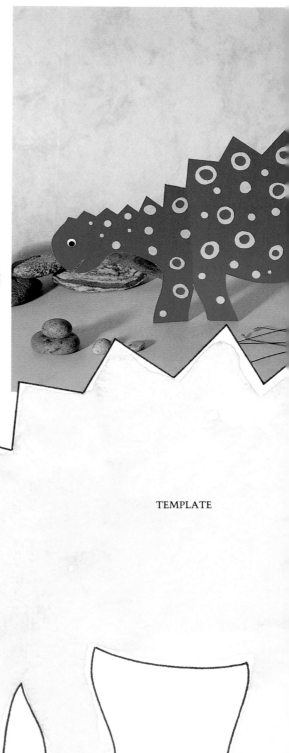

TEMPLATE

2 Score along the fold lines on alternate sides of the card so that the card can fold into a concertina shape. Stick the card to a rectangle of green shiny paper of the same size. Press down well.

3 Copy the dinosaur template on to the card rectangle, matching up the corresponding fold lines. Cut out around the design outline.

4 To make the dinosaur's spots, cut circles and ovals in varying sizes from green and yellow card: make large and small yellow circles and medium-sized green circles. Do not worry if the shapes are irregular, as this will add to the dinosaur's charm.

5 Glue the spots at random over the dinosaur shape, layering the different colours on top of one another. Avoid sticking the spots over the fold lines, as this will make the card rather difficult to fold.

6 Finally, make an 'eye' from a small circle of white paper, topped with an even smaller circle of black paper. Glue this in position.

> **Note:** *A collection of dinosaurs would make attractive table decorations for a children's party. Make a different coloured design for each child to use as an eye-catching place marker. As an alternative to stick-on spots, you could use felt-tip pens or crayons to draw brightly coloured scales or other patterns.*

Dinosaurs capture the imagination of all children, so what better than to give a card shaped like one of these giants!

Sleepy lion puppet card

Children will be delighted with this entertaining card. The lion is made from coloured felt, and is just big enough to slip over small fingers.

REQUIREMENTS
Brown and beige felt
A sheet of thin cream card or art paper
   (Canson paper)
Green crêpe paper
A small piece of thin yellow card or art
   paper
Clear craft adhesive
Double-sided sticky tape
A black felt tip pen
A coin to make a sun template

To make the finger puppet

1   Copy all the template pieces on to felt, choosing beige for the mane, and brown for the body, or vice versa.

2   Run a thin line of adhesive around the edges of one of the body sections, leaving the lower edge clear. Match this to the other body sections, and press to stick.

3   Stick the lower front part of the lion's mane to the body front. Turn the puppet over and stick the back mane section in place, lining up the edges with the front mane.
4   Using the picture as a guide, mark on the lion's eyes, nose and mouth with a black felt tip pen.

To assemble the card

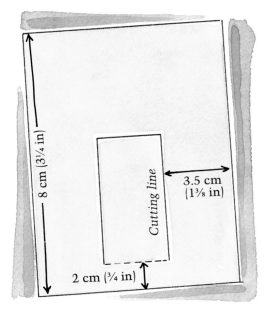

1   Cut a rectangle 20 x 15 cm (8 x 6 in) from cream card. Score a fold line halfway along the longest sides to make the fold.
2   Make a flap over which to slot the finger puppet. To do this mark a line 2 cm (¾ in) from the base of the card. Mark a second line 8 cm (3¼ in) from the base edge. Join the two lines together, 3.5 cm (1⅜ in) in from each side. Cut along the two long edges and the top edge.
3   From green crêpe paper, cut a strip 30 x 4.5 cm (12 x 1¾ in).
4   Place a piece of double-sided sticky tape along two thirds of one of the long edges of the crêpe paper. Remove the backing paper from the tape and fold the crêpe paper into three, to make a strip 10 x 4.5 cm (4 x 1¾ in). (N.B. Do not substitute adhesive for the sticky tape, as the moisture could stretch the crêpe paper, or make the colour run.)
5   Snip along the length of the crêpe paper to make 'grass' shapes.
6   Stick double-sided sticky tape across the lower part of the card, and press the crêpe paper 'grass' to this. Trim the edges.
7   Make the 'sun' by drawing a small circle on to the yellow card. Stick the circle to the top left-hand corner of the card. Trim away the excess. Make the sun's 'rays' from strips of yellow card and stick in place.
8   To finish, slip the finger puppet over the flap cut into the card.

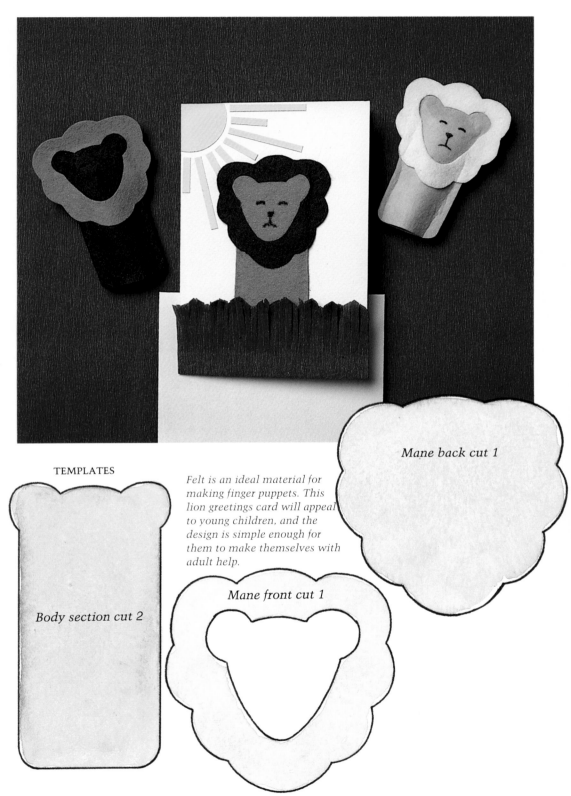

TEMPLATES

Felt is an ideal material for making finger puppets. This lion greetings card will appeal to young children, and the design is simple enough for them to make themselves with adult help.

Mane back cut 1

Mane front cut 1

Body section cut 2

Moving home

Slip this card in the post, to give friends or new neighbours a warm welcome when they arrive at their new home. This sophisticated design is easy to make, and owes its impact to the clever play of light and shadow created by cutting, scoring and folding the card in different directions.

REQUIREMENTS
A sheet of thin card
A small craft knife
Clear craft adhesive
*(See the **Basic Techniques** chapter, page 88 for details on origami symbols and folds)*

1   Cut a rectangle 24.5 x 14.5 cm (9¾ x 5¾ in) from thin card.
2   Mark the position of the fold line in pencil, halfway along the longest edge. Do not score along the line yet.

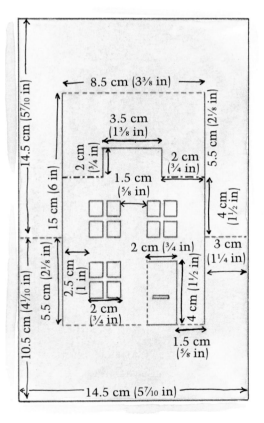

3   Using the diagram as a guide, mark the position of the folding and cutting lines. The 'cutting' lines are indicated by a complete

line, the valley fold lines are marked with a dotted line, and the mountain fold lines are marked with a line of dots and dashes.
4   Cut out the window and letter box sections first. Next, cut or score along the other lines as directed.
5   Carefully shape the card into an upright position by folding, gently but crisply, all the scored lines in the correct direction. Open the door panel so that it stands ajar.
6   To make the roof section, draw a triangle in matching card with sides measuring 9 x 6 x 6 cm (3½ x 2¼ x 2¼ in). Add a chimney to the right-hand side, and cut out.

7   Stick the roof section to the small flap at the top of the house, making sure that the lowest edge of the triangle is in line with the top edge of the house.

> **Note:** *If you cannot resist adding a decorative touch, stick some patterned giftwrap behind the windows to make blinds or curtains, or add a number to the front door. To send the card, prepare all the folds and bend the card to shape. Then flatten the card and place it in a large, envelope for the post. The card will easily fold back into shape.*

This impressive house card is based on origami folds. Make one in a colour of your choice and add a matching envelope.

Bon voyage

Bid farewell to friends with this clever little card. The jaunty boat is constructed from a series of origami folds, and boasts two sculpted paper sails. Quilled birds and cut-out waves demonstrate more papercraft skills!

REQUIREMENTS
A sheet of white art paper (Canson paper)
Thin patterned giftwrap, or origami paper
A small piece of blue art paper (Canson paper)
A small piece of red art paper (Canson paper)
A cocktail stick
Self-adhesive foam pads
A small length of 3 mm grey quilling paper
Clear craft adhesive
A coin to make a cloud template
*(See the **Basic Techniques** chapter, page 87 for more information on origami).*

To make the origami boat base

1 Cut out an accurately measured 15 cm (6 in) square of giftwrap.
2 With the wrong side of paper facing towards you, fold all four corners into the centre. Then fold the top and bottom folds to the middle of the paper.
3 Fold the left and right-hand sides to the middle.
4 Crease along the diagonal marked lines, as indicated.
5 Now pull out the two arrowed points and flatten them to make a shape the same as the one in the next diagram. Repeat for the other side.
6 Fold the sides together to form an origami boat base.

To assemble the card

1 Cut a rectangle, 23 x 16 cm (9 x 6¼ in) from white paper. Mark and score a fold line half way along the longest edge of the paper. Fold in half to make the card base. Working with the card folded and, starting at the top centre, draw round a coin to shape the top of the cloud. Work two more curves each side of the top curve, placing each one level with the one on the opposite side. Cut out through both layers of card.
2 From blue paper, cut a strip measuring 11.5 x 3.5 cm (4½ x 1⅜ in). Cut a wavy line along one of the longer edges. To form the

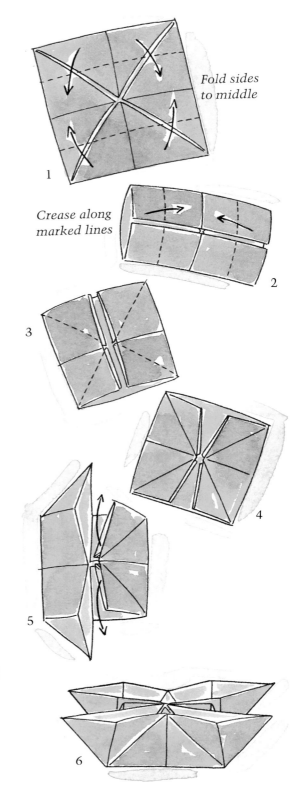

Fold sides to middle

1

Crease along marked lines

2

3

4

5

6

waves, use a craft knife to cut away random small sections from the card. Stick blue paper in place on the card.

3 Stick small pieces of self-adhesive foam pad between the boat base sides, to hold them in shape.

4 Stick a cocktail stick at the centre of the boat, placing the tip just inside the origami shape, to form a mast.

5 Cut two triangles from red paper, cutting one slightly smaller than the other, to make the sails. Gently stretch the edges

of each sail over scissor blades to curve the shapes slightly. Fix them to the card with self-adhesive foam pads, to give a 3-D effect.

6 To make the seagulls, cut three 3 cm (1¼ in) strips of grey quilling paper, and fold them in half. Gently curve the loose ends outwards to make wing shapes. Stick each one to the card, circling above the sails.

A cloud shaped outline adds a finishing touch to this card which shows both origami and paper sculpture techniques.

Happy birthday cake

Surprise the birthday boy or girl with a cake that looks good enough to eat! The cake is actually made from plastic modelling clay, but the real decorations and foil baking case help to create a different impression.

REQUIREMENTS

Plastic modelling clay (Fimo) in white and yellow
Rolling pin (or use a bottle)
Candle holder and candle
Corrugated silver paper (or concertina-pleat some plain silver paper)
Paper cocktail mat
Textured silver paper
A sheet of thin white card
Cake decorations ('Hundreds and Thousands')
Spray adhesive and clear craft adhesive

To make the cake

1   Make the modelling clay more pliable by rolling it in your hands until it is soft.
2   Roll out the yellow modelling clay until it is thin on a clean, smooth surface. Cut a rounded 'cup-cake' shape into it with a knife or pastry cutter.
3   Roll out the white modelling clay in the same way. Cut the curve shape at the top to match the yellow, and cut the lower edge to look like runny icing.

4   Place the white 'icing' on top of the yellow 'cake', and trim the edges to fit if necessary. Cut a small curve into the top of the 'cake' for the candle holder.
5   To harden the modelling clay, follow the manufacturer's instructions, and bake the 'cake' in an oven as recommended.

> **Note:** *You could adapt this card for Christmas by making a plum pudding-and-custard card from brown and yellow modelling clay; add darker 'currants', and substitute a 'plate' for the foil case. Top the design with a fake holly sprig.*

To assemble the card

1   Cut a rectangle 24 x 14 cm (9½ x 5½ in) from thin white card. Score a fold line halfway along the longest side.
2   Cut a rectangle of textured silver foil to the same size, and stick this to the white card with spray adhesive.
3   Cut across the paper cocktail mat about two thirds of the way up to give an illusion of perspective, and trim its lacy edges if necessary. Stick the mat to the lower half of the card front.

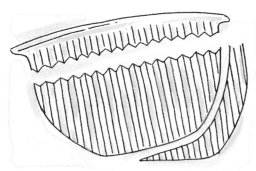

4   Cut a baking case from corrugated silver paper, so that it fits across the lower part of the cake. Cut a zigzag along the top edge.
5   Stick the cake shape to the card, so that it 'sits' on the cocktail mat. Stick the foil case on top of this.
6   Apply a thin layer of clear adhesive to the white 'icing'. Sprinkle 'Hundreds and Thousands' over this. Leave to dry, then shake off any excess.

7   Carefully cut the candle holder in half vertically, using a sharp craft knife. Cut off the pointed end at the base of the holder.

Versatile plastic modelling clay is shaped like an iced sponge cake, and used with real cake decorations to make this witty birthday card.

8 Use clear adhesive to stick the candle into the holder. Trim the back of the candle slightly, where it fits into the holder, so it is level with the cut edge. This will allow the candle to lie flat against the card.

9 Stick the candle and holder on top of the card. The candle will stand in relief above the top edge of the card – so, if anyone gets the urge to light the candle, the card, and all your hard work, will not go up in smoke!

Country-style roses

Tiny ribbon roses in a hessian 'basket' make a pretty subject for a card, and soft colours and rich textures add to its charm. The matching bow trim adds a finishing touch.

REQUIREMENTS
A sheet of thin, white textured card
A small piece of hessian
Nine ready-made ribbon roses
A length of sheer fabric ribbon to tone with the roses
Clear craft adhesive

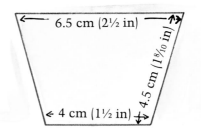

1 Cut a rectangle 22 x 13 cm (8½ x 5¼ in) from thin white card. Score a fold line halfway along the longest edge.

Ribbon roses are available from haberdashery department, but you can also make your own from strips of narrow ribbon.

2 Cut a small piece of card to make the basket, as shown in the diagram.

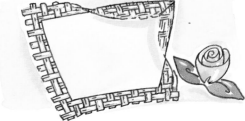

3 Cut a piece of hessian slightly larger all round than the card basket. Join the two together, folding the edges of the hessian to the back of the card.
4 Stick the basket to the front of the card.
5 Make a large bow from the sheer ribbon, and stick this on to the basket front.
6 Starting at the top of the basket, stick the ribbon roses to the card, bunching them together neatly above the basket.

Good luck

Make this striking black cat to send as a good luck charm for someone special.

REQUIREMENTS
A sheet of thin black shiny card
Shiny self-adhesive white paper (or substitute shiny white paper and spray adhesive)
A black pen

1   Cut a rectangle 22 x 13.5 cm (8½ x 5¼ in) from black card.
2   Mark a fold line halfway along one of the long edges. Score along the fold on the inside of the card.

3   Copy the template on to the card. Cut around the cat outline through both thicknesses of card (front and back), as far as the top of the mat. Colour round the cut edge with a black pen.
4   Lightly mark the base outline of the cat on to the front of the card.
5   Mark a chequered mat design, made from 1 cm (⅜ in) squares, on to both the card and the white paper. Score through the marks on the white paper, so that the top layer is cut through, but the backing paper is still intact.
6   Peel the white squares from the backing paper, and position them on the front of the shiny black card.

A black and white cat is a good luck token. Add a shamrock, or a tiny silver horseshoe to the corner of the card for extra luck!

Fold

Base centre

The template only shows the cat and half the card base. Reverse the tracing for the other half of the base.

Chapter 3
With love

Sweetheart

A large sugar-pink heart covered with a shower of pale violet mini hearts offers a traditional Valentine love token. Victorian-style paper scrap cherubs and paper lace trim add to the card's sentimental charm. Add a sprinkling of scent for extra effect.

REQUIREMENTS
A sheet of thin, pale pink card
A sheet of thin, dark pink card
Scraps of thin, shiny mauve card
White paper doilies
A wad punch or belt-hole punch
Victorian-style paper (découpage) scraps
Clear craft adhesive.

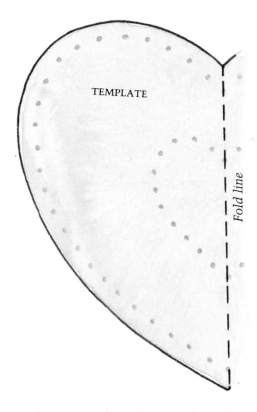

TEMPLATE

Fold line

1   Cut a 28 cm (11 in) x 14 cm (5½ in) rectangle from pale pink card. Score a fold line halfway along the longer edge.
2   Using a pencil, draw a large heart on the front of the card, about 1.5 cm (¾ in) in from the outer edges.
3   Cut the outside lacy edge away from one or two doilies, and gather this lightly into even pleats.

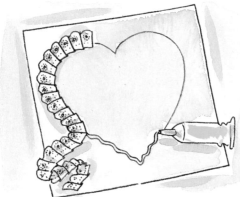

4   Run a thin line of adhesive around the heart outline. Gently pleat and stick the lacy pleats along this line, easing the pleats round curves and angles as you go, and keeping to a good 'heart' shape.
5   Cut a dark pink heart the same size as the first one drawn on the card.

6   Use a punch to make small holes around the edge of the heart, just within the outline. Punch out a second small heart in the centre of the heart.
7   Stick the heart to the front of the card, making sure that all the inside edges of the paper doily are covered.
8   Cut tiny hearts from mauve card and fix them with a tiny dab of adhesive in the centre of the heart, and between the punched hole pattern.
9   Cut two cherubs from a sheet of découpage scraps. Use a dab of adhesive to attach one on each side of the card, at the base of the heart.

The Victorians made Valentine cards popular, and this design borrows their favourite motifs for a modern greetings card. Soft colours complement the sentimental theme.

Valentine hearts

Give Valentine's Day some passion and drama – really broadcast your affections with this richly embellished Valentine card – the recipient would find it difficult to ignore this bright, bejewelled card. The basic card is shaped to form two hearts entwined.

REQUIREMENTS
A sheet of thin red card
A red felt square
Red sequin trim
Gold foil tissue paper
Red and gold plastic gemstones
Spray adhesive and clear adhesive

1   Cut a rectangle 22 x 16 cm (8½ x 6¼ in), from red card. Mark and score a fold line halfway along the longest edge.
2   Copy the heart template on to the card, matching the fold lines. Fold the card in half and cut around the design outline, through both card thicknesses.
3   Using spray adhesive, stick the red felt to the front of the card. Cut around the heart-shaped outline. Cut the two slots for the arrow to pass through.

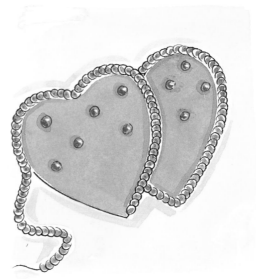

4   Trim the outline of the two hearts by sticking sequin braid round the edges. Decorate the felt surface with red and gold gemstones, stuck randomly over the surface. Dab adhesive on the backs of the sequins and use tweezers to drop them in position.

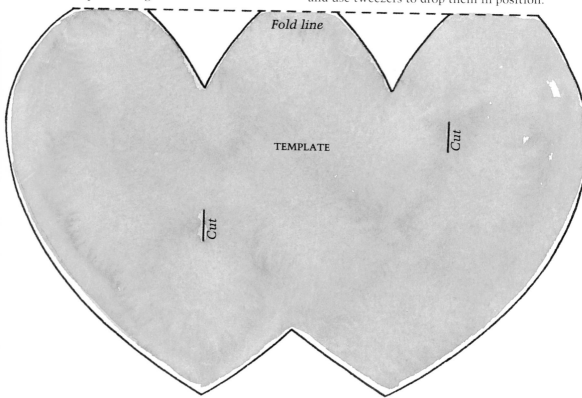

Fold line

Cut

TEMPLATE

Cut

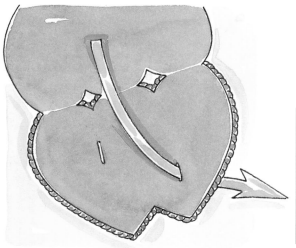

long (or longer as desired), with an arrow head at one end. Thread this backwards through the slots cut in the front of the card.

6 Cut two small hearts from gold paper and stick them to the end of the arrow.

7 To finish, decorate the arrow and the small hearts with a few red gemstones.

> *Note: Deliver your Valentine card in style, by making an envelope to complement the design. Choose bright red paper for the basic shape, then place a miniature bejewelled arrow across the flap to seal. If the card has to be sent by post, omit the arrow and decorate the envelope with 'jewels' cut from metallic giftwrap.*

5 To make the Cupid's arrow, stick gold foil tissue paper to a piece of card. Cut a strip 6 mm (¼ in) wide by 17 cm (6¾ in)

This richly embellished Valentine card uses dress trims imaginatively. The fold line at the top of the card is hidden by a line of sequins.

Sorry!

Make a card to say sorry to somebody special. This sad little bear would appeal to all age groups, and could be used for all sorts of messages – 'Sorry you're leaving'; 'Sorry I missed you'; 'Sorry, I forgot your birthday' – the possibilities are endless! All you need to make the card are some felt scraps and oddments of lace and ribbon.

REQUIREMENTS
A sheet of thin cream card
A piece of thin brown card
Brown felt
Fawn felt
Scraps of black felt, lace and ribbon
Two small black beads
Spray adhesive or clear adhesive

1   Cut a rectangle 22 x 14 cm (8½ x 5½ in) from cream card. Mark and score the fold line halfway along the longest side.
2   Mount the felt on to card with adhesive. This will give the felt motif a little extra support.
3   Copy the various parts of the teddy bear pattern on to the card backing on the brown and fawn felt. Check to make sure that you have the following from brown felt: one complete bear motif and one head, and from fawn felt: two feet and two foot pads, two inner ears and one paw. Cut out all the pieces.
4   Stick the felt bear motif to the lower, left-hand corner of the card, close to the fold line.
5   Using the picture as a reference, position and stick the rest of the bear pieces on to the bear motif.
6   Make the bear's nose and sad-looking mouth from an oddment of black felt.
7   Stick two small beads in place for eyes.
8   Make a small bow tie from a piece of ribbon, and add a handkerchief made from a lace scrap folded into a triangle.

> **Note:** *You could create a different look with a patchwork bear. Stitch small fabric squares together, bond them to interfacing, and cut out the bear.*

The little bear motif could be scaled up or down to decorate a large card or a tiny gift tag or, he could look cute on a bookmark.

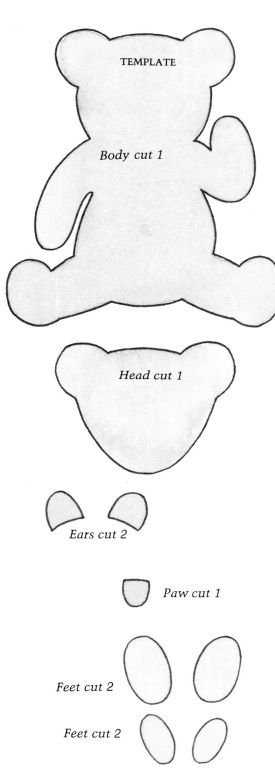

TEMPLATE

Body cut 1

Head cut 1

Ears cut 2

Paw cut 1

Feet cut 2

Feet cut 2

Mother's day

This pretty wreath of pressed flowers would delight any mother on her special day. Gardens in spring and summer display a wealth of flowers and foliage for you to press; pick them then and keep a stock pressed ready for making beautiful flower picture cards to give to friends and family.

REQUIREMENTS
A sheet of thin watercolour card
An assortment of pressed flowers and
 foliage
A flower press
Tweezers
Small, old artist's paint brush (do not use a
 good brush as the adhesive will ruin the
 bristles)
Small stationery fastener, gold stud or flat-
 backed gem
Ribbon bow
Clear adhesive
(See the **Addresses and Stockists** *list at the back of the book for mail order pressed flowers)*

1 Cut a rectangle measuring 28 x 16 cm (11 x 6¼ in) from the watercolour paper. Mark and score the fold line halfway along the longest edge.
2 Look at your collection of pressed flowers and leaves, and plan a basic layout in your mind before handling the delicate plants. A simple bouquet or circle design will suit most 'ingredients'. Then, practise positioning the chosen pressed flowers and foliage on a spare piece of paper cut to the same size as the finished card. Use tweezers to pick up the delicate pressed flowers, taking care to handle them gently as they can be rather brittle.
3 Once you are satisfied with your overall design, start transferring the flowers to the card mount. Work with one flower or leaf at a time, using the tweezers to manoeuvre each one into position. Use a small artist's paint brush to dab a tiny spot of adhesive on to the back of each flower and leaf. Then place in position.
4 Continue in this way until you have transferred all the flowers and foliage to the card to make up your complete design.
5 To make the design look like a 'real' picture, push a stationery fastener into the card, about 2.5 cm (1 in) above the design.

Make a small ribbon bow as a finishing touch, and fix it to the card just beneath the fastener with adhesive.

Pressed plant material

If you do not already have a selection of pressed flowers and foliage, you will need to press some at least one week before you plan to use them.

To do this, pick a selection of flowers and foliage in varying shapes and colours, choosing only those that are in peak condition. If you do not have enough plant material of your own, ask friends and neighbours if they can help. Once picked, arrange the flowers separately between two sheets of smooth textured, absorbent paper, such as blotting or lining paper. Avoid using tissues as they may stick to the plant material and ruin all the carefully chosen items. Press foliage in exactly the same way.

If you do not have a proper flower press, place the layers of paper and foliage between the leaves of a heavy book – a telephone directory is ideal for this purpose. Weight the book down with more heavy objects and leave in a warm, dry place for at least a week. The pressed materials can be stored indefinitely in this way, until you require them to make a card or picture. Stored like this, they are less prone to damage.

Alternatively, if you do not have access to any plant material suitable for pressing, or do not want to press your own, it is possible to buy a limited selection of pressed flowers and foliage from some card-mount suppliers.

Note: Pressed flower cards are usually regarded as keepsakes because of the preparation and meticulous care required to produce the finished design. With this in mind, why not present a picture frame – thoughtfully chosen to fit the card – as an accompanying gift!

'Pansies for thoughts' are part of the language of flowers, so these pressed pansies are a good choice for a special greetings card.

Chapter 4
Congratulations

Lovebirds

This thoughtful wedding or engagement design is a variation of the familiar three-fold card. The bird motif is cut through two layers of card, and backed with net for a see-through effect. Layers of confetti are trapped inside, to create a translucent image. Try adding a really special touch to a wedding card, by making it in colours to complement the bride's or bridesmaids' dresses.

REQUIREMENTS
A sheet of thin, pale pink card
Pale pink net fabric
A box of confetti
Spray adhesive

1 From pink card, cut a rectangle measuring 34.5 x 15 cm (13½ x 6 in). Mark three fold lines along the length of the card at 11.5 cm (4½ in) intervals to make a three-fold card. Score along the fold lines. Trim 3 mm (⅛ in) from the edge to be folded inside the card, for a neat fit.
2 Copy the dove design on to the centre section of the card, making sure that it is positioned the right way up for folding. Carefully cut out all the sections.

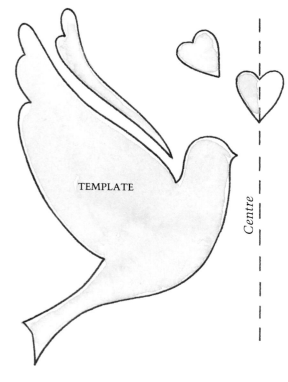

TEMPLATE

Centre

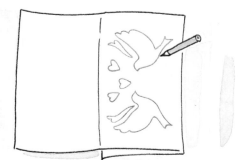

3 Fold-in the trimmed side of the three-fold. Trace through the cut-out on the centre section to transfer the image on to the folded-in section of the card. This will ensure that the cut-out sections line up. Open the card out and cut around the design outline.

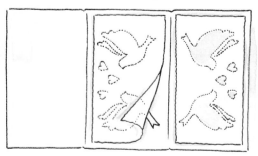

4 Cut two pieces of net measuring 14 x 10.5 cm (5½ x 4¼ in). Protecting the uncut section of the card with some scrap paper, spray adhesive on to the wrong side of the two cut-out sections. Fix the pieces of net in place – to cover each side of the cut-outs.

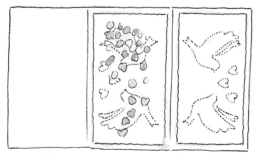

5 Spray a small amount of adhesive on to the net (protect the remaining card section as before), and sprinkle confetti all over this. Then spray a little more adhesive over the area and press these two net-covered sections together to form the finished card.

The cut out birds and hearts design is backed with net and coloured with confetti.

Golden anniversary card

This classic card has been specially coloured to celebrate a golden wedding anniversary but it could be coloured silver or ruby.

REQUIREMENTS
A sheet of thin white card
Gold acrylic paint
A small piece of sponge
A small artist's paint brush
Stencil manilla or acetate (alternatively, use a piece of ordinary card)
Masking tape
12 cm (4¾ in) narrow gold ribbon
A wad or hole punch

1 Cut a rectangle 24 x 14 cm (9½ x 5½ in) from white card. Mark and score the fold line halfway along the longest edge.
2 Transfer the motif of the bell and ribbon on to the stencil card or acetate. Using a sharp craft knife, cut out all the sections accurately, taking care not to cut any other part of the card.

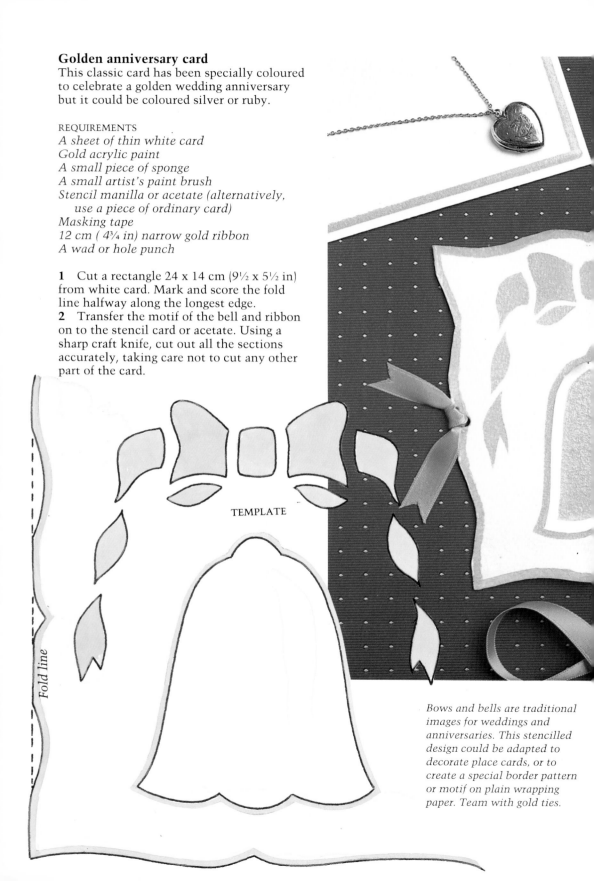

Fold line

TEMPLATE

Bows and bells are traditional images for weddings and anniversaries. This stencilled design could be adapted to decorate place cards, or to create a special border pattern or motif on plain wrapping paper. Team with gold ties.

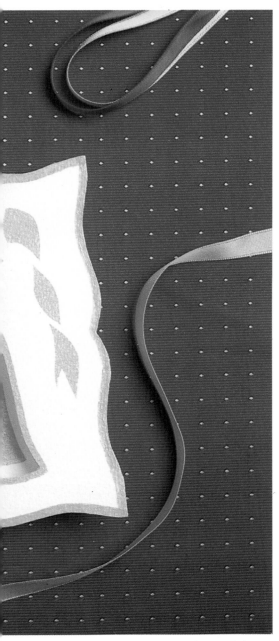

completely fill-in the cut-out sections. Leave the paint to dry before removing the stencil, to prevent smudging the design.

6   Using a sharp craft knife and, following the pencil outline, cut out the bell section from the card front.

7   Fold the card in half along the scored line, and use a sharp pencil to indicate the position of the bell on the inside of the card.

8   With the inside of the card facing, position the bell part of the stencil on the right-hand side, using the pencil marks as a guideline. Sponge paint the bell area only this time. Remove the stencil when dry.

9   Use scissors to cut a fluted edge around the three open edges of the card. Now cut a fluted edge along part of the folded edge of the card, but leave the middle and two end sections uncut.

10   Using the paint brush, add a narrow gold border round the outside edges of the card, by following the fluted outline. Paint an imitation fluted edge to match, along the folded edge. Finish off by painting a thin gold border around the cut-out edge of the bell on the front of the card.

11   Punch a small hole through both card thicknesses in the middle of the folded edge. Thread the ribbon through, and tie in a knot. Trim the ribbon ends into points.

3   Position the stencil on the front of the card, to the right of the fold. Secure in place with masking tape.

4   Mark the position of the bell in pencil.

5   Stencil-in the ribbon area of the motif only, with a little gold paint on the sponge. Use a gentle dabbing action for the best effect. For a subtle, mottled effect, sponge the area lightly; for a stronger effect,

Baby bootees

Enchant any proud new parents with a pair of these cute little bootees. They are quick enough to make as soon as you hear of the new arrival. The folded card is cut into a bootees silhouette, and a pretty little needle-pricked pattern gives them an authentic look. Baby ribbon threaded across the tops, simply adds to their charm.

REQUIREMENTS
A sheet of thin pink or blue card
A medium-sized sewing needle
An eraser
A length of white ribbon 7 mm (¼ in) wide
Clear craft adhesive

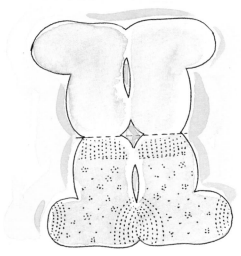

1 Draw the template twice on to the pink card, reversing the template at the fold line as indicated. Cut out and score along the fold line.

2 Mark a line 2 cm (¾ in) down from the fold line. Mark a second line 8 mm (⅜ in) above the first line.

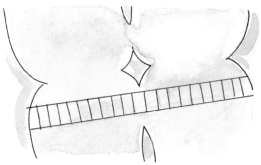

3 Starting 3 mm (⅛ in) in from each edge, and working between the two lines, mark slots 5 mm (⅕ in) apart, all the way across the top of the bootees (there should be twenty slots in total). Cut out. These slots form the holes through which the ribbon is to be threaded.

4 Weave a 20 cm (8 in) length of ribbon through the slots in the card, leaving an equal amount extra at either side. Fold the loose ends to the inside of the card and stick neatly across the back of the slots.
5 Make two ribbon bows and stick them in place along the middle slots at the top of each bootee.
6 Follow the template pattern to prick a design on to the bootees, using a sharp needle embedded into an eraser 'handle'. Work the design shown here, or select a pattern for yourself. The card is now ready.

> **Note:** *It would be a good idea to decorate an envelope made to fit the card with a pricked-pattern outline or motif – perhaps some miniature bootees.*

The lacy pattern on these bootees is quickly worked with a sewing needle. Copy the pattern here, or create your own design.

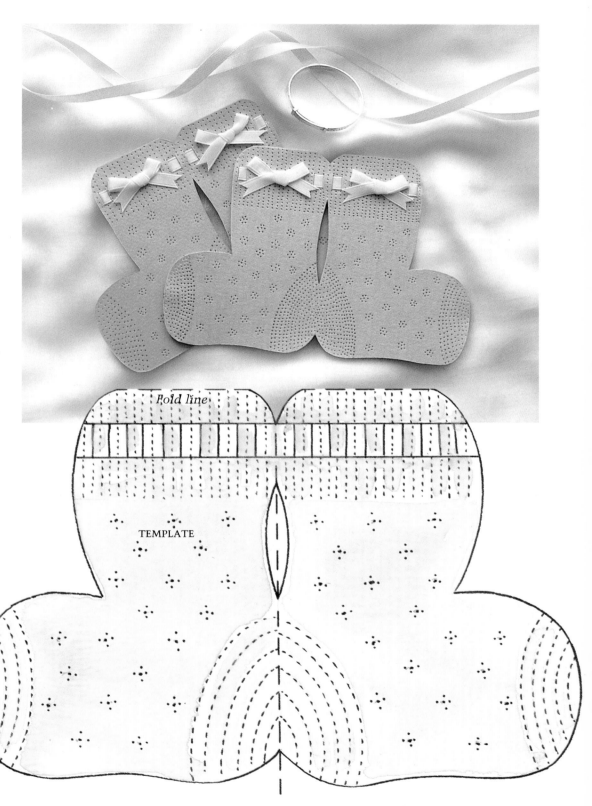

Fold line

TEMPLATE

Well done!

The passing of an important examination or test is a cause for celebration and so what better way to mark the occasion than by making a congratulatory scroll! In order to present this unusually shaped card in the best possible way, a special container (made from a cleverly disguised cardboard tube) is an absolutely essential accessory.

REQUIREMENTS
A sheet of thin watercolour paper
A tea-bag (optional)
An elastic band
A length of (red) ribbon
Sealing wax (gold, silver or red)
A coin (or similar sized object with a relief pattern)
A cardboard tube with a 4.5 cm (1¾ in) diameter
A sheet of giftwrap
Spray adhesive and stick adhesive

To make the card

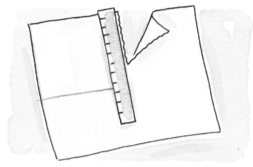

1   Draw a 19 cm (7½ in) square on to watercolour paper, positioning the borders so that you retain as many of the 'rough', unfinished edges as possible. Do not cut the card. Instead, to give it a more 'antique' appearance, place a metal rule along the drawn outline and tear the paper along this.

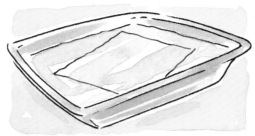

2   If you wish to 'age' the paper further, use a little cold tea to tint the surface of the paper, to give it a faded, yellowish appearance. To do this, either dab a damp tea-bag over the entire surface, especially along the edges; or soak the whole piece of paper in a shallow container filled with cold tea. Once you have achieved the desired effect, leave the paper to dry thoroughly.
3   Roll up the paper to form a cylindrical, scroll shape. Hold it in place with an elastic band. (Make sure that it is not so tight that it marks the paper.)

4 Cut a 12 cm (4¾ in) length of ribbon. Wrap this around the middle of the scroll and stick the ends together to form a loop. Remove the elastic band. Cut another piece of ribbon 15 cm (6 in) long. Fold this in half at a slight angle and stick it in place over the join of the first ribbon.

Presenting an 'antique' scroll, complete with wax seal, is a fun way to offer congratulations to someone who has just passed their exams.

5 Melt a generous amount of sealing wax on to the ribbon join. Press the coin into the wax while it is still warm, to make a seal.

To make the container

1 Cut the cardboard tube to measure 23 cm (9 in) long. Lightly score two half-circle shapes at each end of the tube, and bend these inwards, to produce closed fastenings (see diagram). Then open out the ends again.
2 Cut a rectangle of giftwrap 28 x 16.5 cm (11 x 6½ in). Spray adhesive on to the reverse side of the paper and wrap it around the cardboard tube, leaving a 2.5 cm (1 in) overlap at each end.

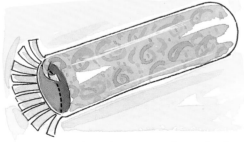

3 Snip into the giftwrap overlap at both ends, and then push the snipped edges down into the tube. Secure with stick adhesive.
4 When you are ready to send the scroll card, simply pop it into the special cylindrical 'envelope' and bend the edges in at each end to seal the card safely inside.

Chapter 5
Invitations

Origami summer invitation

An origami butterfly, folded from softly marbled paper, adds a delightful finishing touch to this summer party invitation. The swirling patterns of the marbled paper give life to the crisply folded origami shape and complement the creamy yellow of the background papers.

REQUIREMENTS
A sheet of thin yellow card or thick paper
Metal ruler
Craft knife
A sheet of marbled paper/giftwrap
A sheet of thin cream card or thick paper
Clear craft adhesive and stick or spray
   adhesive
*(See the **Basic Techniques** chapter, page 88*
for more information on basic origami
symbols and folds)

To make the butterfly

Cut an accurate 10 cm (4 in) square from marbled paper.

1   Make horizontal and vertical mountain folds and diagonal valley folds across the paper as shown.

2   Fold the square in half, plain sides together. With your thumb on the centre of the unfolded outer edge, lift the right half of the paper and open it out to form a triangle.

3   Press the triangle flat, then lift the left-hand wing across to lay on top of the right wing.

4   Repeat these steps for the other half of the shape to make a complete triangle shape.

5   With the point of the triangle facing downwards, fold the point along the dotted line to meet the top edge.

6   Fold the bottom corners along the dotted lines and then unfold them to form a crease line.

7   Fold the inner corners in again along the crease line made in the last step.

8   Fold down the front triangles by pulling down the topmost outer corners to the bottom centre as shown.

9   Make a mountain fold along the centre of the butterfly. Press this as flat as possible to form a sharp fold. Now crease each side of this line to form a V shape. Fold in place to form the butterfly shape.

10   To help the butterfly keep its 3-D shape, use adhesive to stick the upright body sections together to form a peak.

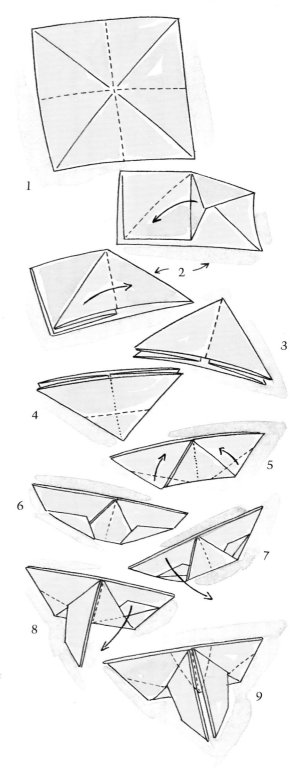

A butterfly made from a folded square of paper adds an unusual touch to an invitation. You could make smaller butterflies from matching paper to decorate an envelope.

To assemble the card

1 Cut a rectangle 12.5 x 12 cm (5 x 4¾ in) from thin yellow card. Mark a border 1 cm (⅜ in) in from the outer edge, and mark an inner border 1 cm (⅜ in) in from this. Within this border measure and mark narrow slits so that strips of marbled paper

can be woven under these. Start at each corner, placing the first slits at right angles.

2 Using a metal ruler and craft knife, score and then cut the marked slits.

3 From marbled paper cut four 12 x 1.5 cm (4¾ x ½ in) strips. On the wrong side of the paper lightly score lines 3 mm (⅛ in) in from each side of the long edges. Fold the paper to the wrong side along these lines to form strips 9 mm (³⁄₁₀ in) wide. Repeat for each marbled strip.

4 Carefully weave the paper through the border slits, making sure that the paper sits on the right side of the card at each corner.

5 When all the strips have been woven into the border, neaten the ends if necessary, and then fold the ends under one another to form neat corners.

6 Use scissors to cut a soft, wavy edge around the outer edge of the yellow card.

7 From the cream card, cut a 13.5 x 13 cm (5¼ x 5¹⁄₁₀ in) rectangle. Stick this to the back of the yellow card. Cut round the edges, following the outline of the yellow card, to form an outer border.

8 Decide on the position for the origami butterfly, and stick in place.

3-D découpage place setting cards

3-D découpage enables you to create intricate-looking and elegant card designs very quickly and easily. The floral motifs used for these attractive place markers were cut from sheets of giftwrap and from ready-made découpage scraps.

REQUIREMENTS
A sheet of giftwrap with a repeat motif (or three identical découpage scraps)
Scissors
Spray adhesive
A sheet of white paper (typing or copy paper)
A sheet of thin white card or thick paper
Double-sided sticky foam pads
*(See the **Basic Techniques** chapter, page 89 for more information on working 3-D découpage)*

1   Decide which motifs to use from the giftwrap and cut out three identical shapes, leaving a generous border round each one.
2   Spray the reverse side of each motif with adhesive and stick them on to the sheet of white paper.

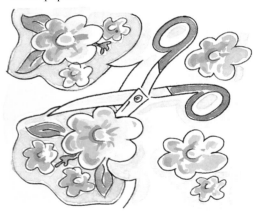

3   Carefully cut round the entire outline of the first motif. From the second and third motifs cut out certain details that you wish to highlight, such as a cluster of tiny flowers, or an upturned petal. By doing this you will gradually build up enough details to produce a 3-D effect when the components are assembled.
4   From the white card, cut a rectangle to measure at least double the height of the complete motif plus 1 cm (⅜ in), and as wide as the motif plus an extra 4–5 cm (1½–2 in).

5   Shape the place setting card by scoring a line across the centre to mark a fold line. Use scissors to create a soft, curvy edge.

6   Stick the complete motif to the bottom corner on one side of the card, leaving adequate space to write the guest's name.

7   Place a few sticky pads (cutting them into smaller pieces if necessary) on to the reverse side of the second motif details. Carefully position these over the first motif, lining up their corresponding outlines. Repeat for the third motif, building the image up in layers to produce a realistic looking picture.

> *Note: Self-adhesive foam pads are used for quickness and convenience to layer the paper motifs. 3-D découpage is also often worked with a clear silicone sealant.*

The designs on these cards are created by placing a number of identical paper motifs together in layers to create a 3-D effect. Self-adhesive foam pads secure the motifs.

Apple invitation card

This amusing apple-shaped invitation is ideal to send for lunch dates, or a picnic-style party. Make large and small apple cards, and use the little ones for place markers. The card is a simple cut-away design, with the apple tops and leaves cut out in relief along the fold line of the card. Choose bright colours for the best effect.

REQUIREMENTS
A sheet of thin white card
A sheet of thin red card
A sheet of thin green card
(or art papers such as Canson or cover
paper)
Clear craft adhesive

1 From white card, cut a rectangle measuring 17 x 12 cm (6¾ x 4¾ in). Mark the fold line in pencil halfway along the longest side, but do not score the fold line.

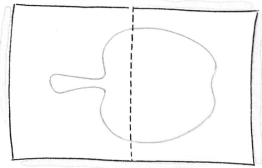

2 Trace the apple template, minus the leaves, on to the rectangle so that the top of the apple projects 2 cm (¾ in) above the marked fold line, so that most of the apple is on the lower side of the fold.

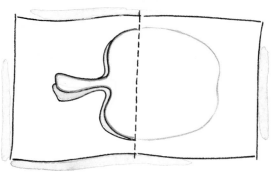

3 Carefully cut out those areas of the apple (the top and the stalk) that project above the fold line. Do not cut out the rest of the apple shape – this will be covered with red.

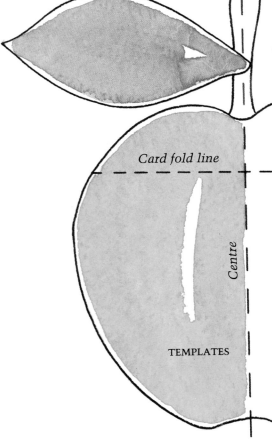

Card fold line

Centre

TEMPLATES

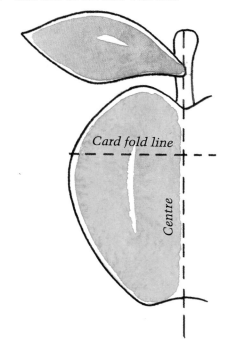

Card fold line

Centre

5 Cut the apple shape, minus the stalk and leafy parts, from red card. Cut two leaves from green paper.

6 Stick the red apple on to the corresponding area of the white card. Stick one end of each leaf on to the stalk.

> **Note:** *To make matching individual place settings, just reduce the size of the template and follow the same steps as for the invitation card, reducing the size of the card appropriately. The place setting shown here was made from a rectangle measuring 10 x 8 cm (4 x 3¼ in).*

4 Score along the fold line on each side of the cut apple shape, without scoring across the shape itself. Fold the card along the scored line – the top of the apple and the stalk are now in relief above the fold.

The same apple and leaf motif has been used to decorate a card and a place setting marker. The motif would also make a good gift tag.

Something special

The beauty of this invitation card, with its delicately pleated motifs and intricate filigree scrolls is that it could be used for almost any occasion – albeit a special one!

REQUIREMENTS
A sheet of thin, pale pink card or art paper
    (Canson paper)
A sheet of toning, mottled pale pink paper
A sheet of toning, marbled pale pink paper
A quilling tool and a sewing needle
Clear craft adhesive and spray adhesive
*(See the **Basic Techniques** chapter, page 90*
for more information on quilling)

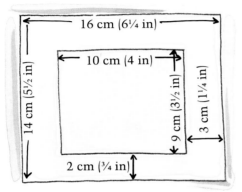

1 Cut a rectangle 16 x 14 cm (6¼ x 5½ in) from pink card. Draw another rectangle 10 x 9 cm (4 x 3½ in) inside the first rectangle, positioned 3 cm (1¼ in) in from the top and two sides, and 2 cm (¾ in) in from the lower edge. Cut this out with a craft knife.
2 Cut a rectangle 16 x 14 cm (6¼ x 5½ in) from marbled pink paper. Stick the thin card border to the front of this paper rectangle with spray adhesive.

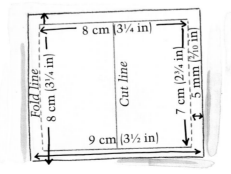

3 Cut a second rectangle 9 x 8 cm (3½ x 3¼ in) from thin pink card. Lightly mark an inner rectangle, 5 mm (¼ in) inside this, to measure 8 x 7 cm (3¼ x 2¾ in). Cut along the two longer edges.
4 Measure the halfway point along the two cut 8 cm (3¼ in) lines. Cut a line down this centre point to form two 'doors'. Score along the two uncut shorter edges to open.
5 Stick this small rectangle on to the front of the card, positioning it 5 mm (¼ in) in from the border.
6 Turning to the back of the card, hold the card up to the light source (or a lamp), and prick a zigzag pattern through the thin marbled paper strip, which should just show between the two thin card areas.

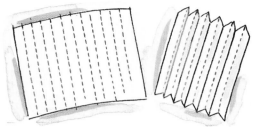

2   Mark along the long edge of each rectangle at 5 mm (¼ in) intervals. Fold up into concertina pleats.
3   Pinch the smaller concertina shapes together at the centre. Secure with a small dab of adhesive between each fold to make 'bows'.
4   Take the large concertina shape, and stick the lower edges of each fold together. Join the two side edges of the top pleat up together to form a fan shape. Do this by overlapping the edges and sticking them in place.
5   Stick the large fan to the top of the card. Then stick the smaller pleated 'bows' around the card border.
6   Cut twelve strips 15 cm x 3 mm (6 x ⅛ in) from pink marbled paper to make filigree scroll shapes.

Three delicate shades of pink paper are used to make this impressive invitation card. Quilled paper scrolls, crisply pleated bows and pricked paper lace create the decorative effects.

7   Cut a rectangle 16 x 14 cm (6¼ x 5½ in) from thin pink card. Use spray adhesive to stick this to the back of the existing rectangle, to form a protective backing for the card.

The decorations

1   From the pink, mottled paper, cut one rectangle 12 x 10 cm (4¾ x 4 in) and eight small rectangles 10 x 2.5 cm (4 x 1 in).

7   Mark the halfway point along the length of ten of the strips. Using a quilling tool, roll each strip up to the halfway point in one direction, and release. Repeat with the other halves, but roll them in the opposite direction, to form scrolls.
8   To make the door 'handles', quill the remaining two strips in one direction only. Secure the ends with a dab of adhesive.
9   Stick the quilled shapes to the 'doors'. Stick the 'handles' in position, then arrange the other shapes so that they balance well, as shown in the picture.

Party mania

'Stepping out', 'Sharp dressing' and 'Cheers!' are a collection of invitation cards with a strong graphic image. They would make a very good gift as a 'boxed set' of cards, as the different designs complement one another so well. Black and white papers with a glossy sheen, and versatile sequin trim are used to great effect.

Cheers!

Add a sparkle to someone's day with this jazzy cocktail card. The ingredients are metallic giftwrap and shiny mirror card mixed with a dash of black sequin trim.

REQUIREMENTS
A sheet of thin, silver mirror card
A sheet of red iridescent giftwrap
Black sequin waste trim
Spray adhesive
Hole punch with choice of hole size

1   Cut a rectangle 24 x 16 cm (9½ x 6¼ in) from silver card. Score a fold line on the reverse side, halfway down the longest side.
2   To make the cocktail glass, cut a large triangle and a smaller triangle from black sequin trim. Use the pattern formation of the holes to help you make the shapes. Cut a piece of thin black border from one edge of the sequin trim, and stick each end to the triangles to make a stem for the glass.
3   Spray adhesive on to the reverse side of the sequin triangles, and stick them on to the red iridescent giftwrap. Trim around the edges to match the sequin trim, to make a red and black cocktail glass.
4   Stick this to the front of the silver card, positioning it at an angle, from the left-hand corner of the card.
5   Cut circles in varying sizes from the red iridescent giftwrap, and stick these to the front of the card to form a cascade of bubbles.

A picture of a cocktail glass suggests a party, and this one is brimming over with fizz. The imaginative use of shiny card, giftwrap and versatile sequin waste create a dramatic image.

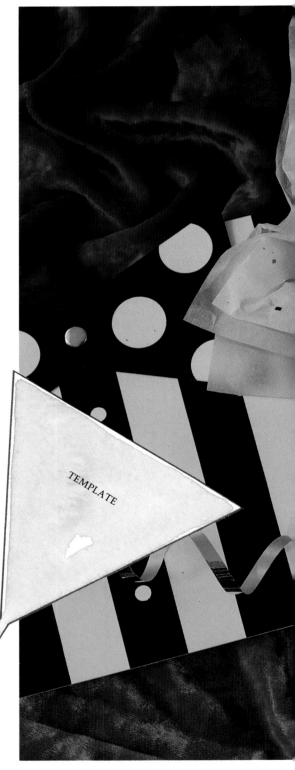

TEMPLATE

Stepping out

High-heeled shoes and a flirty bow suggest a party. The card is cut so that the top of the shoe stands in relief above the fold line, which emphasises its dramatic shape. The bright red bow adds a risqué finishing touch!

REQUIREMENTS
A sheet of thin white card
A sheet of white, glossy, self-adhesive paper (or glossy white paper and spray adhesive)
Black sequin waste trim
Narrow, shiny red ribbon
Spray adhesive
Clear craft adhesive

1   Cut a rectangle 18 x 16 cm (7 x 6¼ in), from both the thin white card and the glossy white self-adhesive paper. Join the two rectangles together.
2   Mark the position of the fold on the card side, halfway down the longer side – but do not score along this line yet.
3   Transfer the shoe template on to a spare piece of card and cut out.
4   On the card side of the rectangle, and working on one side of the fold line only (the card front) pencil in a border 1 cm (⅜ in) in from the lower edge and sides.

5   Position the shoe template within the border, so that its outer edges (toe, heel and shoe back) touch the border lines. Draw around the areas at the top of the shoe that extend over the fold line. Remove the template.

6   Carefully cut round the outline of these marked areas. Then score along the parts of the fold line that do not cross over the shoe area.
7   Carefully fold along the scored line. The top, cut parts of the shoe should stand in relief above the fold line.

8   To make a piece of sequin trim large enough to cover the shoe shape it may be necessary to join two strips together, by carefully butt-joining the edges. Lightly spray the back of a length of sequin trim with adhesive, and position over the template. Repeat to cover the shape as necessary. Cut around the template, and remove it from the sequin trim.
9   If necessary, spray a little more adhesive on the back of the sequin trim, and then position it on the front of the card, taking care to line up the top, cut-away sections of both edges. Press flat to stick.
10   To finish, make a small red bow, and stick it in place on the front of the shoe with clear adhesive.

> **Note:** *If you prefer, you could substitute the red shiny ribbon trim on the shoe front with a diamanté button or a bow made from sheer black ribbon. Alternatively, add a gold stud – any of these variations will complement the design perfectly.*

This party shoe sits cleverly on the shiny white background so that it forms a silhouette above the top fold line of the card. The shoe itself is shaped from black sequin waste.

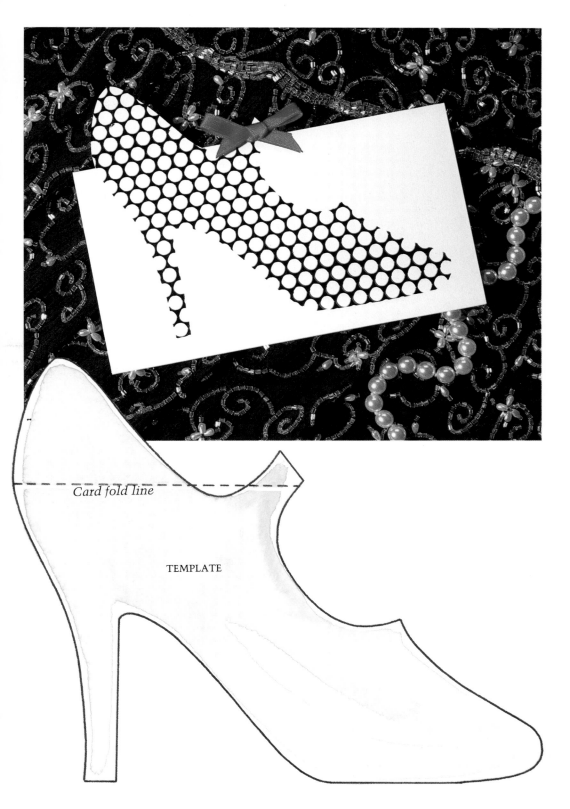

Card fold line

TEMPLATE

Sharp dressing

Black and white spots and flashy stripes combine to create a snazzy bow tie and shirt, and a perfect invitation card for the boys. This card has been made from patterned giftwrap paper, but the same effect could easily be achieved using shiny black and white paper.

REQUIREMENTS
A sheet of thin white card
A sheet of black and white striped giftwrap
A sheet of black and white spotted giftwrap
A stationery fastener
Scraps of white, self-adhesive paper
A hole punch
Spray adhesive

1 Cut a rectangle 30 x 14 cm (12 x 5½ in) from thin white card. Score to fold halfway down the longer side.
2 Stick the rectangle to a piece of black and white striped giftwrap, making sure that one of the black stripes runs vertically down the centre of the long edges. Trim the paper to match the card.
3 Cut a bow tie from a rectangle of card measuring 12 cm (4¾ in) wide by 7 cm (2¾ in) high.
4 Stick the tie shape to the spotted giftwrap, making sure that the spots on each side of the tie are symmetrical. Trim round the edges.

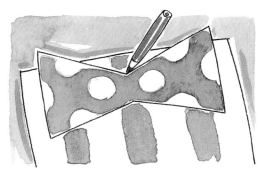

5 With the card folded, place the bow tie on the front of the card, 1 cm (⅜ in) in from either side, and 5 mm (¼ in) above the fold line. Mark the position of the centre point at the top. Remove the bow tie.

6 Mark 2 cm (¾ in) in from each side along the fold line. Join these points to the point marked for the centre of the bow tie. Cut out along these lines.
7 Pierce a small hole in the middle of the bow tie, and a corresponding one on the card front, so that the top edges of the tie and the cut-out shape match. Push the stationery fastener through the hole in the bow tie, and fasten it to the front of the card.
8 Punch four circles from white adhesive paper. Stick these on to the centre black strip for buttons.

TEMPLATE

Note: *If making the card from plain papers, use one of the colours as the background and cut the other one into stripes and spots, and make up the design as a collage.*

A striped shirt and spotted bow tie design have great impact in black and white, and the colours look great for a party invitation. Change these, perhaps by substituting a plain shirt and patterned tie or vice versa, for a different 'male' occasion such as his birthday.

Chapter 6
Seasonal greetings

Easter lamb greetings

Woolly lambs are a well-loved springtime image, and this one, made from small balls of scrunched-up tissue paper, has lots of charm. This cut-away design uses texture to full advantage. The 'grass' is made from spiky, snipped strips of paper, and the spring flowers, like the lamb, are from tissue paper.

REQUIREMENTS
A sheet of thin white card
Black, white, orange and yellow tissue
*   paper*
Green paper
Clear craft adhesive

1   Cut out a rectangle 24 x 16 cm (9½ x 6¼ in) from white card. Mark the fold line halfway along the longest side, but do not score along it yet.

2   Copy the outline of the lamb on to one side of the rectangle. The lamb's back should rest along the marked fold line, with the top of its head projecting above this.

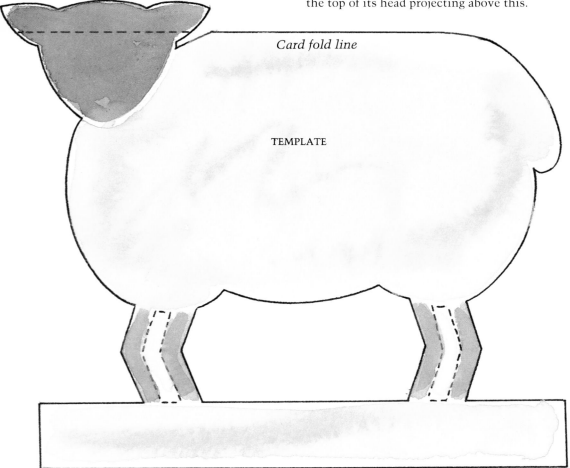

Card fold line

TEMPLATE

3 Cut around the part of the head that is above the fold line. Then score along the remaining fold line.

4 Fold the card in half. Cut around the rest of the design outline, working through both thicknesses of card at the same time.

5 Cover the lamb shape with balls of scrunched-up tissue paper. To make these, simply roll small pieces of tissue paper between your fingers and thumb to make firm, round balls. Try to make the balls of an equal size for each colour. To give a more textured effect, make the white tissue balls for the body about twice the size of the black ones used for the head, legs and tail.

6 Stick the tissue balls to the card, keeping them packed tightly together.

7 Make two tiny yellow balls of tissue, and stick these to the face for eyes.

8 Cut two strips of green paper, one 14 x 3 cm (5½ x 1¼ in) and the other 14 x 2 cm (5½ x ¾ in). Snip all the way along each strip to make 'grass'. Stick the wider strip to the base, followed by the narrower strip on top.

9 Make a row of tiny yellow and orange 'flowers' to add a finishing touch across the base of the card.

Tightly rolled balls of white tissue paper create the fleece on this amusing spring lamb.

Springtime pansy basket

Make this card for someone who loves flowers, and who will admire your skills! The design is a shaped three-fold card, with small sections cut from the front of the basket shape to resemble basketweave. The pansies, cut from giftwrap are applied as quick 3-D découpage and small, green paper leaves set off their shapes. The tissue paper ribbon adds a finishing touch.

REQUIREMENTS
A sheet of thin honey-coloured card
A sheet of thin cream card (or art paper)
A sheet of floral giftwrap, toning tissue
Scraps of thin green card (or art paper)
A sheet of typing or copy paper
Self-adhesive foam pads
Spray adhesive and clear craft adhesive
*(See the **Basic Techniques** chapter, page 89 for information on 3-D découpages.)*

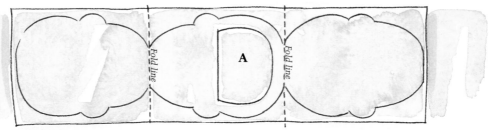

1 Using the template, draw the basket shape on to honey-coloured card three times. Cut out. Cut out the inner 'open' section of the basket (marked A). Score along the fold lines.

Pansy motifs cut from giftwrap are layered to create a 3-D effect in this Easter basket. The card is a basic three-fold design.

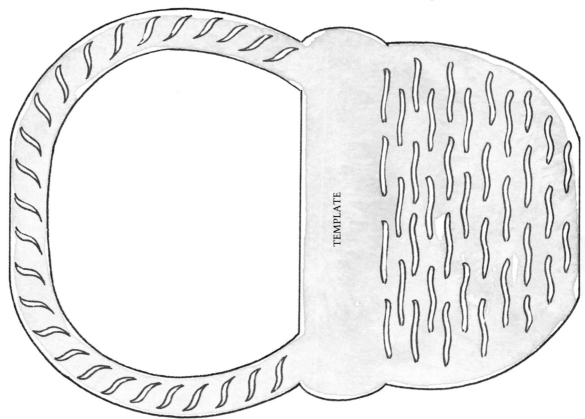

TEMPLATE

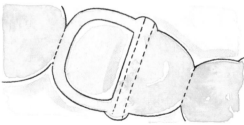

2   To prepare for the ribbon, and working on the centre basket again, draw a line 5 mm (³/₁₀ in) down from the straight edge of the basket. Draw a second line 1.2 cm (¹/₂ in) below the first line.

3   Measure twenty slits 5 mm (³/₁₀ in) apart across the width between these two lines. Cut through the slits.

4   Cut tiny slits across the 'open' basket shape and round the handle to look like basketweave.

5   From tissue paper, cut a strip 18 x 3.6 cm (7 x 1³/₈ in). Divide the width in three and

fold-in the two sides to make the strip 1.2 cm (¹/₂ in) wide.

6   Thread the tissue 'ribbon' through the slits in the card. Turn the ends to the inside and stick in place.

7   Make a bow from tissue paper. Stick this in place over the slits, at the card centre.

8   Draw the basket template on to cream card. Cut out, just inside the drawn outline, to make a basket backing shape that is slightly smaller than the main card.

9   Make a collection of 3-D découpage flowers. Arrange them, and stick them in place on the 'open' (A) marked section on the cream basket. Stick the cream basket behind the main card.

10   Cut tiny 'leaves' from green card and stick these in between the découpage flowers and to overlap the basket top and handle.

11   Fold-up the three-fold card and secure the basket back section with spray adhesive.

Frosty landscape

This ice-cold winter scene is created from a collage of silver foils and textured white papers, and arranged as a simple three-fold card. Glitter paint and glinting silver sequin stars add to the wintry atmosphere.

REQUIREMENTS
A sheet of thin white, textured card
A sheet of textured white tissue paper
Two sheets of silver foil paper, each with a different surface texture
Silver sequin stars
Silver glitter paint
Clear adhesive or stick adhesive

1   Cut a rectangle 51 x 15 cm (20 x 6 in) from thin white card. Score two fold lines at 17 cm (6½ in) intervals along the longest edge, to make a three-fold card.
2   On the centre panel, mark a border 1 cm (¾ in) in from the outside edge – but do not cut out.
3   Within this border, draw peaks across the top half of the card, to form a mountain range. Draw a second zigzag line across the lower quarter of the card, to form a jagged ice effect.
4   Fold the card front (centre rectangle) and fold-in flap card sections together. Then, cutting through both card thicknesses, cut

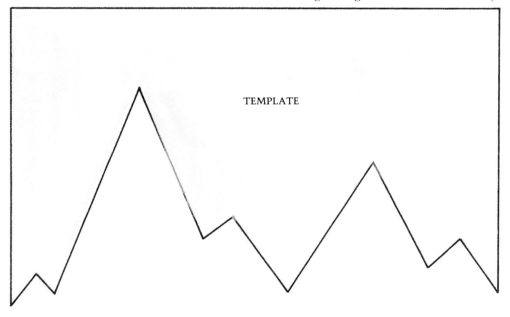

TEMPLATE

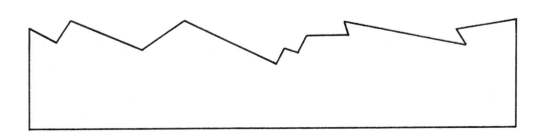

out these marked areas to make cut-out 'sky' and 'water' sections .

5 Cut a rectangle about 14.5 x 5.5 cm (5¾ x 2¼ in) from both the white textured tissue paper and one of the silver papers.

6 Stick these paper rectangles to the inside of the card, so that the tissue paper covers the cut-out above the mountain range, and the silver paper creates the freezing water along the jagged ice edge.

7 Stick the fold-in flap in place over the back of the card front with stick adhesive.

8 Cut some small pine tree shapes from the second silver paper. Stick these in place as desired on the front of the card.

9 Use some silver glitter paint to decorate the mountain peaks with a scattering of 'snow'. Apply this lightly for a subtle effect.

10 Finish off the card by sticking a few sequin stars to the tissue paper 'sky' above the mountain peaks.

Subtle shades of white paper and silver foil create a glistening winter scene.

Christmas cracker

This sumptuously coloured cracker card is designed to hold a handwritten message, or a small but very special surprise gift – a tie pin, some gold charms, a pair of earrings or a ring could all just squeeze into the centre. Undo the fastener to reveal all!

REQUIREMENTS
A sheet of thin white card (or cover paper)
A sheet of thin cerise card (or cover paper)
A small piece of gold giftwrap
A gold paper doily
A sheet of thin typing or copy paper
Two gold-coloured stationery fasteners
A small piece of fine gold giftwrap string
Pinking shears (optional)
Spray adhesive and clear craft adhesive

To make the cracker
1   Cut a rectangle 28 x 6 cm (11 x 2¼ in) from thin cerise card.
2   Mark fold and cut lines along the rectangle, following the measurements in the diagram. Fold to shape.
3   Cut a zigzag edge along each short end of the 'cracker'.

Rich shades of fuchsia and gold create a sophisticated Christmas cracker card.

4   From a doily, cut out a large decorative motif (from the centre perhaps) and six (or more) smaller motifs. Strengthen them by sticking them to a sheet of typing paper with spray adhesive, and cut round the outlines. Cut the large motif in half and stick each half to each side of the cracker's central fold marked (A). Stick the smaller motifs at each end of the cracker, close to the zigzag edges.
5   Open out the cracker shape and pierce a small hole through each large gold motif. Push a stationery fastener through, and bend the ends of each fastener flat at the back of the cracker to secure. Fold to close.

> **Note:** *You can plan the cracker colours to complement the accompanying gift. Make an envelope to match as a finishing touch.*

6   To hold the cracker closed, wind the gold string round the fasteners.

To make the card
1   Cut a rectangle 20 x 16 cm (8 x 6¼ in) from thin white card. Stick this to gold giftwrap and trim to size. Score a fold line halfway along the lower edges.
2   Stick the back, central section of the cracker to the front of the card mount.

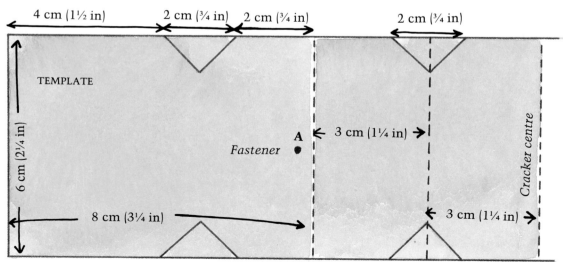

4 cm (1½ in) 2 cm (¾ in) 2 cm (¾ in) 2 cm (¾ in)

TEMPLATE

6 cm (2¼ in)

A

Fastener ●

3 cm (1¼ in)

Cracker centre

8 cm (3¼ in)

3 cm (1¼ in)

Novelty Christmas tree

This festive, free-standing tree is made from two pieces of card, slotted together. A gold star and bead trim provide seasonal cheer.

REQUIREMENTS
A sheet of fairly thick/firm green card
A sheet of thin gold card
Small gold bead trim
A wad punch with small attachment (or use a darning needle)
Clear adhesive

1   Draw each Christmas tree template once on to green card. Cut out. Mark the vertical slot positions on each tree shape, but do not cut along these lines yet.
2   Draw the star template on to gold card to make two stars. Cut out.

3   Stick the two stars to the top of the tallest tree shape, placing one on each side of the card. Make sure that all the points line up, and neaten the edges, if necessary.
4   To make the slots, cut each side of the marked line, to create a slot 2 mm (1/10 in) wide (or to the thickness of the card). Assemble the two tree sections at right angles to each other to form a 3-D shape. If necessary, make any minor adjustments to the slotted sections, so that the base of each tree section lines up accurately with the other side.
5   To add the beaded trim, punch a small hole, large enough to fit the trim, in each of the four tree tips, at the top and third layer of the tree. Thread gold bead trim through the holes in each layer. Join the bead ends together with clear adhesive.

The simplicity of this Christmas tree is part of its charm. An equally attractive tree could be decorated with sequins or paper stars.

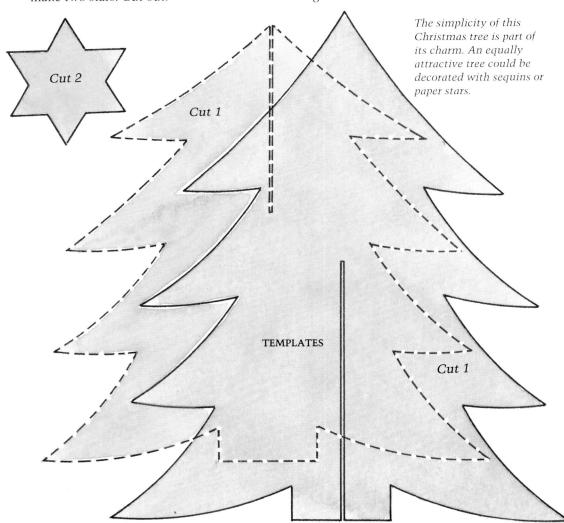

Cut 2

Cut 1

TEMPLATES

Cut 1

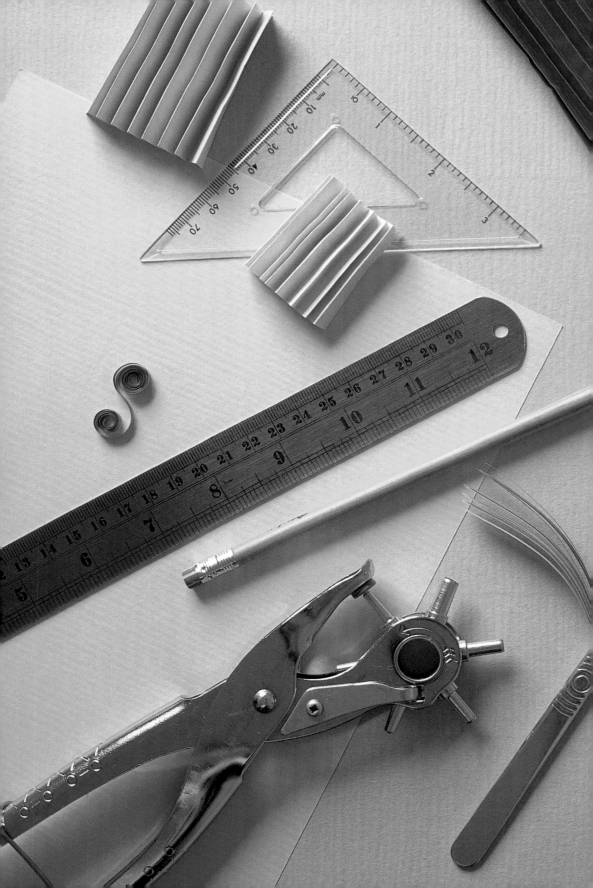

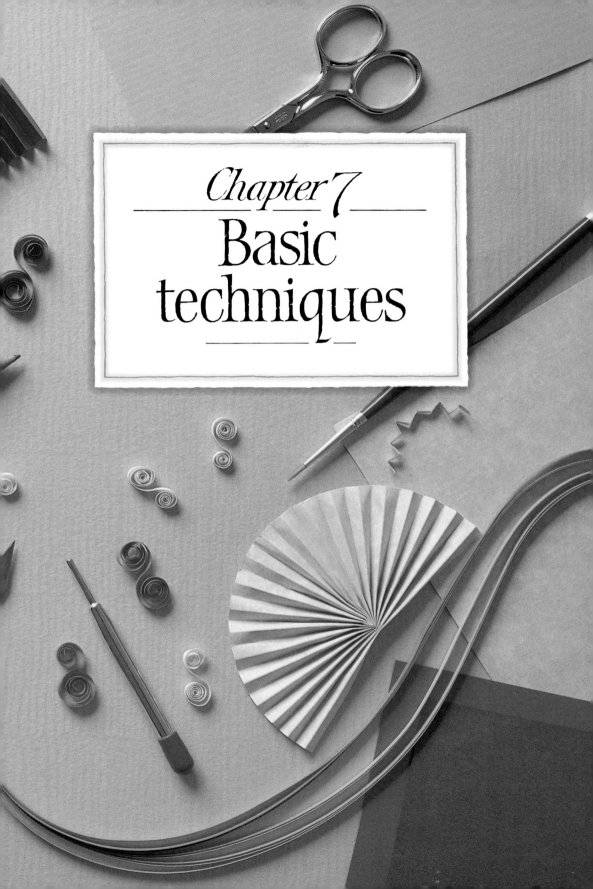

Chapter 7
Basic techniques

Read this chapter to refresh your memory about papercraft skills, or to learn a little more about them.

Measuring and cutting paper and card

When measuring and cutting paper and card always work on a firm, flat surface. For cutting purposes use a cutting board or a piece of thick card. Always work from a straight cut edge to produce accurate measurements. Use a sharp pencil to mark out the shape before cutting; this will help to prevent mistakes being made. When cutting paper or card, use a craft knife or scalpel along the edge of a metal ruler to produce accurate, neat lines and press down firmly on both the ruler and the knife.

Creasing

Before creasing paper by hand, try creasing a small, scrap piece across and along its grain. If the fold line creases easily, the paper can be folded by hand, but if the fold is uneven or broken, the paper is too heavy for hand-folding, and requires an indent to help it fold. This can be done by creasing or scoring the surface.

Lightweight papers would be weakened if scored with a craft knife, so a 'paper folder', or small tool with a pointed, but blunt tip should be used instead. (You can substitute a knitting needle for this, if you have difficulty obtaining a special bookbinder's bone folder.) To crease paper with a paper folder, lay the paper on a smooth, flat surface, and line a straight edge up against the position for the crease. Press down on the straight edge, and with the other hand, run the folder tip along the edge. A gentle indent will be marked, ready to fold.

Scoring

Scoring is a basic technique which enables you to produce very crisp folds and creases in card or paper, which will help your cards acquire a professional-looking finish.

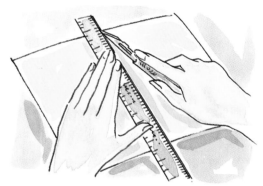

Scoring a fold line involves very lightly cutting the top layer of the surface with the back of the blade of a craft knife, or with a scissor blade held against the edge of a steel ruler. Always score paper and card on the outer, or 'mountain' side of the crease. This is so that the paper can 'stretch' over the fold. With careful and accurate measuring and cutting, scoring will produce a very straight line, making the folding of shapes in card or paper much easier. If, when folded, you find that the two edges of the card are not exactly level, simply trim the edges

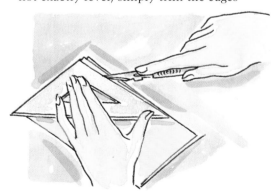

(using a set square for accuracy), cutting through both thicknesses of card at once. Special care must be taken not to score the surface too deeply, which would produce a cut rather than a scored line. Once you have mastered the basic technique of scoring card and paper, you can go on to experiment – you do not have to stick to straight lines; surfaces can be scored in curves or on both sides alternately to give raised surfaces.

Bevelled edges

These are gently sloping angles at the side of a cut piece of card or paper. They are often used on picture mounts, but the technique, cut with either a craft knife or scissors, is useful for many applications when the surface edge requires thinning.

To obtain a bevelled edge when cutting out a detail from a print – as for 3-D découpage – hold the scissors at an angle with the blade against the paper. This thins the cut surface, making it less noticeable.

For thick paper, or card which needs to be cut with a craft knife, hold the knife at a 45° angle to the surface and draw the knife firmly down against a metal ruler.

Concertina pleats

These simple, versatile pleats are formed from accurately marked, equal-width fold lines. They can be made in any size or width you choose, and used to make fan shapes and twists to decorate cards or giftwrap. Choose lightweight and medium-weight papers for the best results. You can shape the paper before pleating into geometric shapes like rectangles, triangles, circles or squares, or you can simply cut a long paper strip into the required width, and pleat this as required. As concertina pleats reduce the original length of the paper by half, make an allowance for this.

To make concertina pleats, use a set square and ruler to accurately mark the pleats across the paper. Carefully measure and mark each pleat position at right angles to one edge, and parallel with the other edge of the paper. Crease the folds as follows:

Concertina pleats on lightweight paper can all be creased from the same side of the paper, but thicker paper should be creased from both sides. For lightweight paper simply run a fold tool along a straight edge held over each marked pleat line.

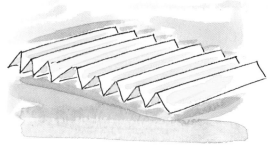

Carefully pleat up the paper, so that the folds go in opposite 'mountain' and 'valley' directions.

Secure the pleats to hold their shape by gripping them in large clips, or wind cord round, until they are required.

For thicker paper, mark the pleats on both sides of the paper (carefully lining-up positions) and crease every alternate line along one side, then turn over and crease the lines on the other side. Shape pleats as before and secure to hold their shape.

Transferring designs

For the best results, designs should be drawn as accurately as possible. If you are given measurements to follow, the shapes can be drawn directly on to the chosen paper or card. Always use very light pencil strokes which can be erased later on.

Tracing designs

If you are working from a template, you will have to transfer the design by hand. This can be done in a number of ways. If the template has been drawn 'same size' then you can simply trace the template, as accurately as possible, and then transfer it to the card using well-worn carbon paper (not erasable) or by re-drawing the image on the wrong side of the tracing paper. Do this, then position the tracing as required, and use a coin to rub over the outline.

Other methods of tracing which exclude the use of tracing paper include placing the required image on a glass-topped table, and putting a table lamp without its shade underneath. The outlines of the design can then be seen clearly, for you to draw round. Alternatively, tape the picture to a window in daylight, and place your paper over this. Tape it securely, and trace-off the design.

Enlarging or reducing designs

If the design needs to be enlarged or reduced you will need to use graph paper to alter the size, or a special tool called a pantograph. This has a special extended 'arm', which can be adjusted to make an enlarged or reduced image when the other end of the tool is traced round the original image.

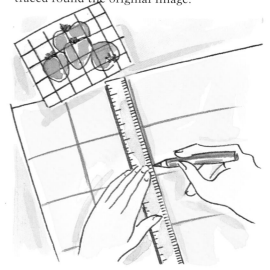

To enlarge a design from a grid, choose squared paper with the required enlarged measurement (or draw a grid yourself to this size, on a sheet of plain paper). Copy the design square-by-square on to the larger grid. Pay particular attention to the positions of drawn lines where they cross over the grid edges, for accuracy.

To reduce a design, just repeat this process in reverse, and transfer the images on to paper with a smaller grid.

A quick way to copy, enlarge or reduce designs is to use a photocopying machine that has all these facilities. However, some degree of distortion may occur.

Different card folds

A selection of ready-cut card blanks and mounts in all shapes and sizes are readily available from art and craft shops, stationers, department stores and by mail order from specialist paper/card suppliers. Alternatively, you can make your own card mounts, ranging from a simple folded card to multiple-fold cards. The card mount can be plain, on to which you add decorations, or you can cut a 'window' in the card, behind which you can trap all types of decorative objects. Choose strong papers or thin card for these designs.

Making a three-fold window card

A three-fold window card is one of the most useful card mounts to know how to make. The following instructions for making a three-fold card can be adapted to make a card with any number of folds:

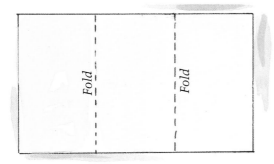

1 Decide how large you want the finished card to be and then draw this size three times. Do this using a sharp pencil to mark the shape (elongated rectangle) on to a piece of thick paper or thin card. Mark the position of the fold lines.

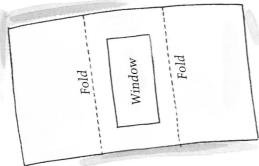

2 Measure the size of the work you wish to mount inside the folded card. Cut an appropriately shaped window to fit. (Squares or rectangles are the easiest shapes to use for windows; other shapes can be used but need to be accurately cut, preferably with a template, otherwise they can look rather disappointing.)

3 Score along the two fold lines on the right side of the card using the back of a craft knife or scissor blade against the edge of a metal ruler. Take care not to cut right through the card.

4 With the right side of the card facing, fold the right-hand flap to the inside of the card. Make sure that the card is not upside down. Open out this flap and trim off between 1 and 2 mm (¹/₁₀ in) from the outer edge, so that the flap will fit neatly inside when the card is assembled.

Envelopes

If you are making your own greetings cards you will need envelopes. Ready made envelopes are available in a range of sizes

from some stationery shops and art and craft shops; they are also available by mail order from specialist card mount suppliers. However, to add a really professional finish to a special occasion, it is quite easy to make an envelope to complement your handmade card. The following instructions show you how to make two very simple envelopes. Alternatively, for unusual or awkwardly shaped cards, such as the scroll congratulations card, where a card tube was used, you will need to use your initiative to make a suitable container in which to present the card.

Envelope 1

1 To make a simple pocket envelope, start by measuring the height and width of the card at its highest and widest points, and adding 6 mm (¼ in) to each side. Following these measurements, draw a rectangle on to a large piece of your chosen paper, leaving plenty of extra space all round for the envelope flaps.

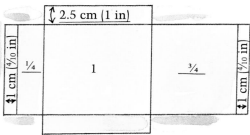

Envelopes made to match or complement a greetings card add a stylish finishing touch. They are simple to make in any size, and can be decorated or trimmed as desired.

2 To work out the size of the rest of the envelope add on the following sizes: at least 2.5 cm (1 in) for each side flap; three-quarters the width of the card plus 1.5 cm (¾ in) for the base flap; a quarter of the width plus 1.5 cm (¾ in), for the top, sealing flap. Using the diagram as a guide, add these measurements to the basic rectangle.

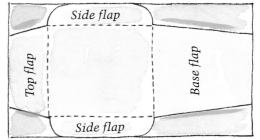

3 Cut out, curving the corners of the side flaps slightly (draw round a coin), and tapering the top and base flaps. Gently score along the dotted lines.

4 To assemble the envelope, turn in the side flaps. Run a line of adhesive along the side edges of the base flap, then turn it up and stick it to the side flaps. When you use the envelope, secure the top flap with adhesive or double-sided sticky tape. Alternatively, for a more ornate finish, use sealing wax to secure the flap.

Envelope 2
1 Measure the folded card generously as before and, following these measurements, draw a rectangle on to a large piece of your chosen paper.

2 To make the top flap, measure and mark the centre of the rectangle. Measure the distance vertically from this centre point to the rectangle outline, and mark this size , adding an extra 1 cm (⅜ in) for an overlap, beyond the rectangle outline.

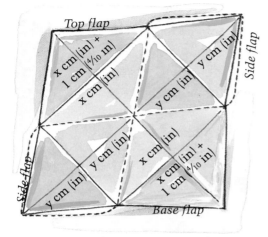

3 Repeat this for the other three flaps, adding the overlap as before.
4 Cut out, and then crease or score the fold lines as necessary. Neatly and accurately fold the side flaps to the inside. Add adhesive to the edges of the base flap, and fold it in to stick to the side flaps. Apply adhesive or double-sided sticky tape to the inside of the top flap, to secure for mailing.

> *Note: Give your envelope design a touch of sophistication by adding a coloured lining. Before assembling the envelope, cut a piece of tissue paper to the same size as the width and length of the envelope, minus the area of the base flap. Secure the tissue with a little adhesive along the edges, and assemble the envelope in the usual way.*

Origami

Origami is the traditional Japanese art of creating 3-D designs from a square of paper without cutting, decorating or gluing the paper in any way. A whole range of shapes can be made simply by following a series of intricate folds. Although origami designs can appear very complex, many are surprisingly simple to make. Many origami shapes are ideal for added decoration on greetings cards, and this book merely touches upon the wide range of shapes it is possible to make; the origami butterfly on a summer invitation card, and a basic multiform shape for the base of the boat on the 'Bon voyage' card are both traditional designs.

There are many books on the popular craft of origami, and these show a wide range of other origami designs that could be adapted to use on cards.

The golden rule of origami is always to fold the paper carefully, accurately and neatly. Good creases make folding easy and help to show the positioning of later folds. To help you achieve successful results, always work on a smooth, level surface; meticulously and neatly measure and cut the paper; make all folds very accurately, running your thumbnail along the crease to make a sharp fold; finally, always follow the diagrams in sequence, looking ahead to the next consecutive step to see what the next shape should look like.

> *Note: If disaster strikes and one or more of the folds goes wrong, don't panic! Carefully check through all the steps one by one to make sure that you have not missed out a vital symbol. If necessary, start back at the beginning again, working slowly and carefully.*

Origami papers

Packs of ready-cut, brightly coloured origami paper are available from specialist Oriental shops, art and craft shops, stationers and toy shops. Although convenient to use, origami paper can be relatively expensive and tends to come in very bright colours, which may not be suitable for the project you are working on. Many other types of paper can be used, providing they are thin, strong and can be given a crisp crease without cracking the surface. Practise folding the shapes on typing or photocopy paper and use giftwrap paper or lightweight art or stationery paper to make the finished design. Avoid using very flimsy tissue papers which do not hold shapes well, or poster paper which tends to crack. Papers can also be folded together if desired, to give a two-colour effect.

Origami symbols include dots and dashes, and these tell you which type of fold to make in the paper. Arrows are used to show the direction of a crease, as well as which way to turn the paper after a fold has been made.

Symbols

A standard system of symbols and terms used alongside illustrated steps makes up the instruction language for folding origami shapes. The following diagrams will help you to understand the few basic symbols necessary to make the origami shapes dealt with in this book.

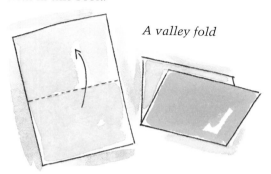

A valley fold

A line of dashes indicates a 'valley fold', which is a simple fold in the paper which, when unfolded, resembles a valley indented into the paper. It is the most common technique in origami and is often referred to simply as a fold or crease.

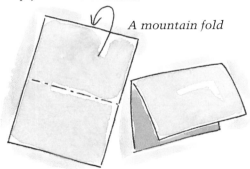

A mountain fold

A line of dots and dashes indicates a 'mountain fold'. This is simply a valley fold worked on the reverse side of the paper to produce a crease that rises up from the paper like a mountain peak.

Arrows are used to indicate the direction in which the paper should be folded. Fold the paper upwards or downwards, right or left, depending on the direction indicated by the arrow.

Self-adhesive foam pads allow you to raise layers of motifs to create a 3-D effect.

Quick 3-D découpage

3-D découpage is a variation of the more familiar technique of traditional flat surface découpage. Small details from several identical patterns are cut out and then arranged in raised layers, separated from one another by self-adhesive foam pads, to gradually build up a three-dimensional effect. The aim is to make background details recede, and give foreground details more prominence. Very realistic-looking effects can be achieved by bevelling and tinting the cut edges of the shapes, and gently moulding the individual motifs before they are stuck in position.

Take into account the scale of the motifs when planning the finished size of the card. Tiny motifs are most suitable for small table place settings; it is best to use larger motifs on large-scale greetings cards, or to cluster smaller motifs together. The finished motifs can be used as a design in their own right, or simply applied as a raised detail in a design.

Materials for 3-D découpage

PAPER: For each 3-D découpage design, you will need at least three identical motifs. Special sheets of découpage scraps, which have repeated designs, are available from craft shops, but it is much easier to use readily available giftwrap papers that have repeated motifs. (For a really co-ordinated look, choose the same giftwrap used for the card to wrap an accompanying present.) Make sure that the motifs have simple shapes with clearly defined outlines that can easily be cut out. For greater strength, you will need plain typing paper to back the design motifs.

ADHESIVE: Use spray adhesive to bond the typing paper to the motifs, and small sections cut from self-adhesive foam pads, to separate and raise the layered motifs. Self-adhesive foam pads are available from stationers and craft shops.

SCISSORS: Use small pointed scissors and manicure scissors for cutting out the motifs.

Cutting and shaping motifs

1   For a professional finish, bevel the edges of the motifs when cutting out. Turn the paper as you cut to produce a smooth edge.
2   Disguise any ugly white edges by carefully tinting them with an appropriately coloured felt tip pen.
3   To make the motifs look more realistic, gently contour each motif by lightly curling the edges over the side of a pencil.

Basic technique for 3-D découpage

1   Cut out three or more identical motifs from the chosen giftwrap, leaving a generous border all round.
2   Spray the back of each motif with adhesive and press flat on to typing paper.

3 Carefully cut around the outline of one complete motif and stick it on to the chosen card mount.

4 Cut out certain details that you wish to highlight from the second motif. Stick a few of the self-adhesive foam pads on to the main motif (cutting them to fit as

necessary), placing them where they will be covered by the second layer. Carefully position these second layer shapes over the first motif, and line up their outlines.

5 Repeat step **4** for the third layer, highlighting even smaller details than before. Fix these in place over the second motif layer.

Quilling

Quilling, or paper filigree, is the art of rolling paper strips into scrolls and coils. These are pinched into different shapes and joined together to build up delicate patterns. The designs can be mounted on to a background or used as free-standing decorations, earrings and mobiles.

Although quilling looks intricate, the shapes are quite simple to make and many people find the action of rolling the paper relaxing. Quilling is surprisingly strong, and finished pieces can be further strengthened with a coat of varnish if desired. Special books of quilling designs are available from craft suppliers, but there is no reason why you cannot create your own designs. Inspiration can come from wrought-iron patterns, mosaics, or from embroidery transfer patterns and book illustrations. You can also make doodles, and copy these.

Equipment
QUILLING TOOLS: Quilling tools of different sizes are available from specialist suppliers, craft shops and some department stores. However, it is simple to make your own range. All you need is a stick with a split at the top to hold the paper while it is coiled. This can be made from a cocktail stick or a large sewing needle with the top of the eye sawn off. The size of the tool affects the finished size of the coil. A pencil or wooden dowel is useful for making very large coils.

Quilling papers
These are sold in colour-blended groups, in pre-selected widths and lengths for easy use. The papers are normally available in metric sizes, in 2 mm, 3 mm and 10 mm widths, and 450 mm lengths. These can be cut or torn to size as required. An average working length is 200 mm. Carnival streamers, or strips cut from giftwrap paper or wallpaper can also be used to create different effects.

ADHESIVES: Use clear craft adhesive or PVA adhesive which does not leave trails, to stick quilling coils in place. Use a matchstick to dab-on the adhesive.
VARNISH: Any varnish suitable for paper can be used to protect the finished work.
SCISSORS: A small pair of scissors is needed for accurately cutting the strips to size.
PINS: These are needed to hold shapes in place when assembling the finished shapes.

Quilled designs are made from loosely or tightly coiled narrow paper strips.

Basic quilling shapes

Some of the easiest quilled shapes to make are those which can be attached to a background surface. Make a test selection of these, so that you get used to the feel of the paper and learn to work to an even tension. You might find that the coils you start with are tighter than the ones you make as you become more practised.

Making a coil

1 Cut a 200 mm (7¾ in) length of paper and rub your finger and thumb across the end to soften and bend it slightly. Now gently roll up the strip, keeping the edges even. The finished coil will spring open when it is released.

2 To make a coil using a quilling tool, slip the end of the strip into the slot on the tool and roll the paper round. Let the finished coil fall free from the end – pulling will distort it.

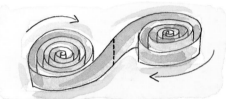

3 To make a scroll, simply coil one half of the paper strip in one direction, release the paper, and roll the other half in the opposite direction.

Tight coils

These are made by rolling up a paper strip and securing both ends so that the coil cannot spring open or unwind. Solid coils are coils with no space in the centre and are made by hand-rolling. To make either, soften and bend the end of the paper as described earlier, and work the coil very tightly. Secure the ends firmly with a dab of adhesive. Tight coils can also be pushed into useful cone or concave shapes.

Useful addresses

The following art stores should be able to supply you with most of your card-making equipment. If you do not have access to any of these stores, your local craft store or newsagent may be able to assist. Ribbons and other accessories are available from haberdashery stores.

Fred Aldous Ltd
P.O. Box 135
37 Lever Street
Manchester 1
M60 1UX
Tel: 061 236 2477
(Mail order supplier of most handicraft materials.)

The British Origami Society
253 Park Lane
Poynton
SK12 1RH
Tel: 0625 872509

Ells and Farrier
20 Beak Street
London W1R 3HA
Tel: 071 629 9964
(Suppliers of fake gemstones, jewels, sequins, beads)

Impress Cards
Slough Farm
Westhall
Halesworth
Suffolk IP19 8RN
Tel: 098681 422
(Mail order supplier of card blanks and pressed flowers/leaves)

Mamelok Press
Northern Way
Bury St Edmunds
Suffolk IP32 6NJ
Tel: 0284 762291
(Suppliers of découpage paper scraps)

Paperchase
213 Tottenham Court Road
London W1A 4US
Tel: 071 580 8496
(Specialist for card/paper, handmade papers)

Past Times
Cumberhills Drive
Duffield
Derby DE6 4HA
Tel: 0332 840582
(Suppliers of quilling materials)

Australia

New South Wales
Will's Quills
164 Victoria Avenue
Chatswood 2067
Tel: (02) 411 2627

Queensland
Eckersleys
91–93 Edward Street
Brisbane 4000
Tel: (07) 221 4866

South Australia
Premier Art
43 Gilles Street
Adelaide 5000
Tel: (08) 212 5922

Tasmania
Artery
137–141 Collins Street
Hobart 7000
Tel: (002) 34 3788

Victoria
Dean's Art
368 Lonsdale Street
Melbourne 3000
Tel: (03) 602 2263

Western Australia
Jackson's Drawing Supplies
103 Rokeby Road
Subiaco 6008
Tel: (09) 381 2488

Index

A
Adhesives, types 14–15
Anniversary card 46

B
Baby card 48
Bevelled edge, how to make 83
Birthday cards 20, 22, 28
Blanks 84
Bon voyage card 26
Bone folder 82
Butterfly card 54

C
Canson paper 12, 18, 22, 26, 58, 60, 70
Card folds, types 84
Card blanks, *see Blanks*
Card mounts, *see Mounts*
Children's cards 20, 22, 28
Christmas cards 74–79
Concertina pleats 83
Congratulations card 50
Craft adhesive 14
Craft knife 14
Creasing, how to 82
Crepe paper 12, 22
Cutting
   how to 82
   tools 14

D
Découpage 56, 72, 89–90
Drawing materials 15

E
Easter card 70
Engagement card 44
Enlarging designs 84
Envelopes
   how to make 85–87
   variations 37, 48

F
Felt 22, 38
Filigree, *see Quilling*
Fimo, *see Plastic modelling clay*
Floral cards 18, 30, 40, 56, 72
Foil papers 36, 74
Folding, how to 82

see also Card folds

G
Gemstones 36–37
Giftwrap 12, 26, 54, 56, 62, 66, 72, 76, 89
Glue, *see Adhesive*
Good luck card 31
Grain, paper 13
Graph paper 84

H
Handmade paper 12
Hessian 30
Hole punch, types 14

IJK
Invitation cards 54, 58–67
Italian paper 12

M
Marbled paper 12, 54, 60
Materials, basic requirements 14–15
Measuring, how to 82
Mother's Day card 40
Mountain folds 88
Mounts 84

N
Net fabric 44
New home card 24

O
Oriental paper 12–13, 74
Origami
   paper 26, 54, 87
   symbols 88
   techniques 87–88

P
Pantograph 84
Paper, sizes and types 12–13
Party invitations 54–55, 62–67
Photocopying 84
Pinking shears 14
Place settings 21, 58–59
Plastic modelling clay 28
Pleating, how to 83

Pressed flowers 40

Q
Quilling
   designs using 18, 26, 60
   papers and tools 90
   techniques 90–91

R
Reducing designs 84
Ribbon roses 30

S
Scissors, types 14
Scoring, how to 82
Scroll card 50
Sequin trim 62, 64
Sheep design 70
Sizes of paper 13
Sorry card 38
Spray adhesive 15
Spray booth 15
Stencilling 46
Stick adhesive 14
Storing paper 13

T
Tape 15
Teddy bear card 38
Templates, how to use 84
Thank you card 18
3-D effects 56, 72, 89–90
Three-fold cards 44–45, 72–75, 84–85
Tinting, how to age paper 50
Tissue paper 12, 70, 72, 74, 87
Tools, basic requirements 14–15
Tracing designs 84
Transferring designs 84

V
Valentine's cards 34–37
Valley folds 88
Varnish, quilling 90

W
Wad punch, *see Hole punch*
Watercolour paper 12, 40, 50
Wedding card 44
Weights of paper 13